Indian Cooking

Lalita Ahmed

Contents

First published in 1981 by Octopus Books Limited
59 Grosvenor Street, London W1

Seventh impression, 1983

© 1981 Hennerwood Publications Limited

ISBN 0 906320 65 8

Printed in Hong Kong

भूमिका

Introduction

The geographic differences of the country's regions have had a marked influence on the eating habits of Indians. In the past, poor transport facilities meant that areas used their own produce and the recipes were developed around what was readily available. The caste system also had a large influence on the styles of cooking. The Brahmins, who were at the top of the four castes, did or did not eat meat, depending on location. For instance those from Bengal ate meat and fish, whereas the Brahmins from the south and north did not. Similarly, the Shatrias (next caste down) did or did not eat meat according to location. The Vasliyas and Shrudras (the last two castes) did eat meat.

Its large population and eating habits mean that India has always had a large number of vegetarians, although nowadays a large number of Indians do eat meat. However the female population still largely remains vegetarian, because they have not travelled and broadened their outlook as much as the men, and adhere more strictly to the rules of their religion.

Meat and poultry dishes became popular with the affluent society during Moslem rule and later on during the British Raj when dishes like tikkia were created. Military invasion and India's trade routes have left a marked foreign influence on meat and poultry cooking – Portuguese vindaloo, and Persian and Greek kebabs and pilafs (pulaos) are examples.

In northern India, which covers Punjab, Kashmir, Uttar Pradesh and Delhi, meat and poultry are widely eaten and from these areas all the tandoori and moghlai dishes originate. The Moslems, Christians and Parsis are all meat eaters and the most famous meat dishes come from the Moslem style of cooking. The methods of cooking meat in the south produce different flavours and use local produce, such as coconut, tamarind and curry leaves. Dishes from the south are hotter and spicier than those from the north. The Bengali (Bangladesh included) method of cooking is extremely tasty and is in a class of its own. The dishes are prepared with meticulous precision and great care. Fried herring, bandhgobhi and dam aloo are some of the specialities of Bengal, but this area is particularly famous for its sweets.

The recipes in this book reflect the different styles of cooking from every region. Always remember that Indian cooking is geared for flexibility. It is not necessary to stick rigidly to a recipe, and when you have tried these recipes and have acquired confidence you can increase or lessen any spice according to taste. As a general rule it is better to make a curry a few hours in advance, as spices take a little time to develop and impart their flavour to the food. Cooked in advance and thoroughly reheated, they are a good choice for entertaining, too.

आयोजन

Preparing the food

When preparing food for Indian cooking it is important to remember a few points.

All the *vegetables* should be of the same size to create a good presentation, and this will also help to ensure even cooking.

All vegetables are first peeled or skinned unless otherwise stated. If not used at once they should be soaked in water to prevent discolouration, especially potatoes, aubergines and carrots.

For curries all *meat* is usually cut into bite-sized pieces.

When all the *spices* for a recipe require dry roasting, they can be roasted together for convenience.

Similarly, you can shorten your work by grinding all the spices for one recipe together. For small amounts of dry spices use a pestle and mortar. For larger quantities an electric grinder is invaluable and often a small quantity of water makes the process easier.

During cooking, food may start to stick to the pan, in which case a little water can be stirred in. Remember though that there are many dry curries, which are not intended to be overly moist and do not have a large quantity of sauce.

To thin down a curry with a sauce, or a daal, stir in a little boiling water.

परोसने की विधि

Serving a meal

These dishes will serve 4–6 people on average, if they are presented in the Indian style. However to serve any of the meat or fish dishes in a Western manner – without offering a selection of side dishes – the quantities may need to be increased accordingly.

Before a meal serve piping hot snacks such as samosas or pakoras with a refreshing sherbet. It is customary to leave a gap of about 45 minutes in between this stage and dinner to encourage a good appetite.

To serve the meal itself put the main dish, such as a biryani or a special roast in the centre of the table and surround it with the other dishes. Although all the dishes are presented and served together, for a formal party a little of each should be kept hot in the kitchen, so that the dishes can be re-filled as required. Both bread and rice should be cooked in ample quantities. It is usual to tear off a portion of bread and use it to scoop up some of the food. Indians frequently eat without cutlery and it is customary to use the right hand only. However the Western approach is to eat with a spoon and fork.

When serving a very moist curry, first pour the sauce into the dish and then arrange the main ingredients. Garnishes are kept very simple, such as a sprinkling of chopped coriander leaves or green chillis.

At the end of a meal serve one or a choice of sweets, followed by tea or coffee. After a meal it is common to serve small cardamom seeds in their husks, aniseeds, or betel nuts wrapped in a green leaf which is called 'pan', as an aid to digestion. To give the whole occasion an oriental touch a mild joss-stick (agarbatti) may be burnt for a few minutes before the meal.

विशेष सामग्री

Special ingredients

Baisen or ganthia flour: A fine yellow flour which is made from ground split black chick peas, and used in many Indian dishes, especially in breads and batters. It is low in gluten and very high in protein.

Pulses (Daals): There are about sixty varieties of pulses available in India. These are the dried seeds of plants such as beans and peas and those most popularly used include chick peas (kabuli channa), split black chick peas (bengal gram or channa), black gram (urid daal), red lentils (arhar) and yellow lentils (moong). Pulses should be rinsed in several changes of water. Pre-soaking usually cuts their cooking time by half and as salt tends to harden pulses it should not be added until the end of the cooking. As they take a long time to cook, a pressure cooker is a great aid to cooking most pulses. The more unusual pulses are sold in health food or Asian food stores.

Ghee (Clarified butter): Ghee can be heated to a higher temperature than most oils without burning and is widely used in Indian cooking. For the best flavour ghee is made from unsalted butter. Cheaper blends of butter are most suitable to make ghee or it can be bought from Asian stores. Once prepared it will keep for up to three or four months in a cool place.
To make 175 g/6 oz ghee, melt 225 g/8 oz butter in a saucepan. Slowly simmer the melted butter until it becomes clear and a whitish residue settles at the bottom. Remove from the heat, spoon off any foam, and allow to cool. Drain the clear oil from the top into a container, straining if preferred. Discard or add the residue to curries for flavouring.

Kewra water: Also sold in the stronger form of essence, kewra water is used for flavouring and has a delicate fragrance.

Rose water: Available from chemists this is used like kewra water for flavouring many Indian dishes. The essence form is more expensive.

Tamarind (Imali): These are the ripe pods of a large tropical tree which are filled with a dark red juicy pulp that has a souring effect. The seeds and pods are discarded. To extract the pulp allow one teacup of hot water to 25 g/1 oz pods. Leave to soak for 10–15 minutes. With the fingers squeeze the pods to release the thick pulp. Immerse the pods again in water for a further 10–15 minutes to extract any remaining pulp. Discard the pods and seeds. Because of its consistency tamarind pulp cannot be made using a sieve.

5

ख़ास मसाले

Special seasonings

Every spice that is used in Indian cookery has a preservative and antiseptic quality and many are considered to have medicinal powers, too. However, their main function is to enhance the flavour of a dish, and if the seasonings are left whole they are discarded as the food is eaten. These more unusual ones are available from Asian food stores or supermarkets.

Aniseed (Sauf): These liquorice-flavoured seeds are widely used in the preparation of liquors, confectionery, sweet and hot chutneys.

Asafoetida (Hing): An ill-smelling medicinal gum resin found in Afghanistan. There are many varieties ranging from light yellow to dark brown in colour but they all have this distinct smell. However, asafoetida has great powers as a digestive agent and for this reason is sprinkled in small, acceptable quantities on vegetable curries, daals, appetizers and chutneys. It is sold in pieces or as a fine powder.

Black Cumin (Shah Zeera): Distinguished from the ordinary cumin variety by its smaller darker seeds which have a stronger but pleasant smell.

Black Salt (Kala-namak): This is rock salt with traces of sulphur in it, which give it a very distinct flavour. A small amount is used to flavour chutneys, chaats and many snacks.

Cardamoms (Elaychi): There are two varieties, large and small. The large variety has a black pod and black seeds inside. The seeds of the small green variety impart a pleasant scented flavour and are mostly used for Indian sweets, pulaos and biryanis. The large variety is seldom used for puddings but both varieties are a main ingredient in the making of garam masala. Unless otherwise specified the cardamoms are used whole and ground with their pods. The ground form is often available in shops.

Chilli (Lalmirch or Mirchi): Available fresh or as powder and in different coloured varieties which range in strength. The seeds are particularly hot and may be removed. Prepare chillis under running cold water, wash your hands immediately afterwards and never allow the volatile oils to touch the face, as they can cause painful stinging.

Coriander (Dhania): In its ground form it is used for ready-made curry powders, vegetable and meat curries, while its green leaves are used for garnishing and for making chutneys. The whole seeds are often included in chutneys, too.

Cumin (Zeera): The seeds resemble caraway but are slightly bitter in taste. Cumin is added to curry powders and garam masala. Whole seeds are used for pulao, vegetable curries and chutneys.

Curry leaves (Curry patta): The green leaves of a tree found in India, Pakistan and Sri Lanka, which are used for flavouring and then removed before serving. Green and dry forms are available.

Dried mango powder (Aam choor): Slices of unripe green mangoes are used in India as a souring agent when lemons, limes and tamarind are not always available. Fresh unripe green mangoes are peeled, stoned, cut into thin slices and dried in the sun, then stored in powdered form, which amongst other uses makes a convenient substitute for tamarind pulp.

Fenugreek (Methi): The yellow seeds are used in curry powders and are slightly bitter. The leaves from the plant resemble clover and are eaten as a leafy vegetable in India. Fresh fenugreek can be grown in a home garden from seed.

Garam masala: For the preparation of dishes ready-made garam masala powder should be purchased from Asian stores. However a little of the following aromatic mixture can be sprinkled on top of a cooked dish, such as curries or kebabs, after serving. To make a garam masala mixture grind 20 small green cardamoms with 8 large cardamoms, 25 g/1 oz cumin, 15 g/½ oz black cumin, 15 g/½ oz black peppercorns, 15 g/½ oz cloves, 15 g/½ oz stick cinnamon, ¼ whole nutmeg, and 4 blades of mace (optional). Store in a sealed jar. The seasonings in this version can be varied according to taste.

Ginger (Adrak or Addu): Sold as ground, fresh root or preserved. Fresh ginger root is sold by weight and will keep in a dry cool place for several weeks.

Ginger and garlic pastes: Since many meat, fish and poultry preparations need garlic and/or ginger paste it is very useful to prepare large quantities of each and store them.

Both pastes can be safely kept with or without refrigeration for 3–4 weeks without change in the taste and flavour. Buy 100–175 g/4–6 oz ginger root or garlic cloves, and peel them. The process is made easier if the ginger is soaked overnight. Chop the ginger into small pieces. Grind the garlic or ginger with the minimum of water necessary to make a fine

Special seasonings: Onion seeds (1); Fresh ginger root (2); Chilli powder (3); Ground turmeric (4); Small green cardomoms (5); Curry leaves (6); Green chillies (7); Saffron fronds (8); Aniseed (9); Garlic cloves (10); Large cardomoms (11); Fenugreek (12)

paste. Add 1 × 1.25 ml/¼ teaspoon salt, mix well and store, wrapped in a polythene bag, and placed in a sealed container. Avoid storing either of these pastes too close to other foodstuffs.

Onion seeds (Kalongi): These are collected from shoots produced by the onion and widely eaten in India in both sweet and savoury preparations.

Rattan-jog: This is the dried bark of a reed-like plant grown in India and used mainly to colour food. When cooked with meat or vegetables a small piece imparts a deep red colour to the dish. It is available in Punjabi as well as certain Asian shops.

Saffron (Zafran or Kesar): Saffron fronds yield a rich yellow colour and an exquisite flavour. Saffron is used as a colouring agent for pulao, biryani, sweets, puddings and cakes. Gathered from the crocus flower, thousands of fronds are needed to produce a very small amount.

To make a solution of saffron for colouring, first wrap the saffron fronds in a small polythene bag and crush with a rolling pin, or use a pestle and mortar. Transfer the saffron to a cup and pour the specified amount of hot water or milk over it. Leave for 10 minutes and stir well with a spoon. For a large pinch of saffron fronds use 50–85 ml/2–3 fl oz water or milk.

Turmeric (Haldi): The saffron-yellow ground form is most commonly used. It is sometimes used to colour a dish but because of its distinctive flavour should only be used when it is in the ingredients anyway.

विशेष विधियां

Special techniques

Colourings: The use of subtle colourings in Indian cooking is commonplace. Saffron and turmeric are often used. However the latter imparts a particular, and sometimes overwhelming, flavour and the former is expensive, so a popular alternative is to make up a weak solution of orange or yellow food colouring.

Dry roasting: Many spices are dry roasted for a few seconds to heighten their flavours. This is best achieved by gently heating either a non-stick or heavy-based frying pan. Add the spices and over a very gentle heat move the spices around the surface of the pan. Because of their pungency, dry roast chillis in a covered pan.

Separating ghee or oil: This stage is often referred to in Indian cooking. It occurs when the ghee or oil comes to the surface during cooking and it is most noticeable when fairly large amounts of ghee or oil are used. It is an important technique as it ensures the best flavour from the spices.

Tempering (Baghar, Phoran, Darka): The terms given to the process in which a seasoning, combined with oil or ghee, is poured over a dish before it is served. The purpose of this is to either add a flavour without incorporating it in the cooking process or to increase the amount of oil.

भोजन का चुनाव

Choosing a meal

Indian dishes are ideal for group eating because rather than preparing one dish per person, several are presented simultaneously. Even on an everyday basis it is usual to offer the family a choice of curries, rice and bread. In total 4–8 dishes may be served and this style of eating 'stretches' easily to feed extra guests. There should be at least one meat, poultry or fish curry and one vegetable dish; choose either a curry or a daal.

When cooking at home, pay particular attention to serving a good balance of dry curries and moister dishes. Avoid serving a meal of either entirely one type or the other. Dry curries can be identified in this book by their titles, although most curries can be adjusted to be either moist or dry.

क्या पियें ?

What to drink

It is usual in India to drink a simple sherbet before a meal and the choice of what to serve with the meal is then largely a matter of taste. It is still fairly unusual to serve alcohol with a meal in India and instead water or fruit juices are served. Carbonated drinks are becoming popular, especially amongst children.

However, if you wish to serve an alcoholic drink light semi-sweet or rosé wines are the best complement to Indian food. Dry white wines are not a good accompaniment to Indian food and avoid drinking any wine with a raita, as the two do not go well together. Lager and beer are popular alternatives.

४ से ६ शाकाहारी लोगों को भोजन भेंट करने के लिये सुझावित मेन्युः

Suggested menu for a vegetarian meal to serve 4 to 6 people:

Menu A
Buttermilk sherbet
Deep-fried bread
Vegetable pulao
Lentil curry
Boondi raita
Spiced aubergine
Potato, pepper and pea curry
Sesame seed and onion chutney
Rice pudding

From the front, clockwise: Leavened bread; Lentil curry; Plain boiled rice; Cucumber raita; Mixed vegetable curry; Meat curry; Milk balls in syrup

४ से ६ लोगों को दोपहर का भोजन भेंट करने के लिये सुझावित मेन्युः

Suggested menus for a lunch or informal dinner to serve 4 to 6 people:

Menu A
Mango sherbet
Plain rice
Leavened bread
Meat curry
Mixed vegetable curry
Cucumber raita
Lentil curry
Milk balls in syrup

Menu B
Spiced grape sherbet
Spiced potato in batter
Traditional curry
Madras mackerel curry
Plain boiled rice
Cabbage curry
Wholemeal bread
Coriander and mint chutney
Yogurt pudding

४ से ६ मेहमानों की दावत के लिये सुझावित मेन्युः

Suggested menu for a formal dinner to serve 4 to 6 people:

Mixed fruit sherbet
Meat-stuffed pastries
Rich bread
Tandoori chicken
Prawn curry with coconut
Okra curry
Vegetable pulao
Mixed vegetable raita
Mango chutney
Chick pea flour fudge

SHERBETS AND SNACKS

Sherbets were introduced by the invading Turks and Persians and were originally consumed in large quantities because they replaced the large loss of body water which occurs in India's tropical climate. For this reason, sherbets are still readily offered as refreshment in India; sometimes with the addition of alcohol. As part of a meal they are served with the snacks.

Snacks are an important part of Indian cuisine. They can be treated as appetizing savouries to be served before a meal with a sherbet, as light dishes for lunch or supper, or they can be used as side dishes for a more substantial meal. The majority of snacks can be eaten hot or cold.

Lassi (buttermilk sherbet)

Metric	Imperial
300 ml plain unsweetened yogurt	*1/2 pint plain unsweetened yogurt*
pinch of salt	*pinch of salt*
50 g caster sugar (or to taste)	*2 oz caster sugar (or to taste)*
1.2 litres water	*2 pints water*
ice cubes	*ice cubes*

To decorate:
grated lemon rind
few mint leaves

To decorate:
grated lemon rind
few mint leaves

Preparation time: 5–7 minutes

Beat together the yogurt, salt and sugar thoroughly. Add the water and mix well. Serve in tall glasses with ice, lemon rind and mint leaves.

Pakoras or bhajias (fritters)

Metric	Imperial
100 g potato, peeled and cut into 3 mm slices	*4 oz potato, peeled and cut into 1/8 inch slices*
100 g onion, peeled and sliced in rings	*4 oz onion, peeled and sliced in rings*
100 g cauliflower florets	*4 oz cauliflower florets*
100 g aubergine, sliced in rounds	*4 oz aubergine, sliced in rounds*
100 g green pepper, sliced in rings	*4 oz green pepper, sliced in rings*

Batter:
120 g baisen flour
pinch of baking powder
about 1 × 2.5 ml spoon chilli powder
salt
about 85 ml water
juice of 1/2 lemon
oil for deep frying

Batter:
4 1/2 oz baisen flour
pinch of baking powder
about 1/2 teaspoon chilli powder
salt
about 3 fl oz water
juice of 1/2 lemon
oil for deep frying

Preparation time: 15–20 minutes
Cooking time: about 30 minutes

Pakoras are deep fried fruit or vegetable fritters. The batter is made with a special flour, called baisen, which is the flour of the channa (chick pea), or bengal gram as it is sometimes called.

Sift the baisen flour, baking powder, chilli powder and salt. Add the water to make a smooth batter. Add the lemon juice and beat well. Set aside.
Heat the oil in a pan until a drop of the batter in the oil rises quickly and turns crisp. Dip the vegetable pieces a few at a time in the batter and deep fry them until golden brown and crisp. Drain on kitchen paper and keep hot while deep frying the rest. Serve hot with tomato ketchup or a chutney.

Variations:
Other sliced fruits and vegetables to use instead are semi-ripe bananas, pineapple, apples, mushrooms, firm tomatoes, or use thickly shredded cabbage or spinach. Also try cubes of cooked chicken or fish.
To make shapes of batter without any filling, make a much thicker batter and add 1 × 5 ml spoon/1 teaspoon cumin seeds.

Lassi; Pakoras

Thandai (milk and saffron sherbet)

Metric
15 g blanched almonds
15 g pistachio nuts
10–12 small green
  cardamoms, shelled
pinch of saffron fronds
50 g caster sugar (or to
  taste)
1.2 litres milk, chilled
1 × 1.25 ml spoon ground
  turmeric
1 × 1.25 ml spoon ground
  nutmeg or 3 drops
  nutmeg essence
crushed ice (optional)

Imperial
½ oz blanched almonds
½ oz pistachio nuts
10–12 small green
  cardamoms, shelled
pinch of saffron fronds
2 oz caster sugar (or to
  taste)
2 pints milk, chilled
¼ teaspoon ground
  turmeric
¼ teaspoon ground
  nutmeg or 3 drops
  nutmeg essence
crushed ice (optional)

Preparation time: 15 minutes

Also known as kesher doodh, this is a very popular Indian refreshment and can be made with hot milk too. In many parts of India a little alcohol is added, and the sherbet is drunk during festivals such as Holi (festival of spring) or Diwali (festival of lights).
The ground mixture may be prepared in a larger quantity and stored in a sealed jar for several months. This flavouring can also be included in puddings and sweets.

Finely grind the almonds, pistachio nuts, cardamoms and saffron fronds. Dissolve the sugar in the milk by stirring thoroughly. Add the turmeric, nutmeg and the ground mixture. Stir well and serve, adding crushed ice if preferred.

Nimbo pani (lemon or lime sherbet)

Metric	Imperial
85 ml fresh lemon or lime juice	*3 fl oz fresh lemon or lime juice*
1 litre water	*1¾ pints water*
50 g caster sugar (or to taste)	*2 oz caster sugar (or to taste)*
pinch of salt	*pinch of salt*
8–10 mint leaves or rose petals, washed	*8–10 mint leaves or rose petals, washed*
ice	*ice*
lemon or lime slices, to decorate	*lemon or lime slices, to decorate*

Preparation time: 10 minutes

Mix the lemon or lime juice with the water. Stir in the sugar and salt until dissolved. Gently crush the mint leaves or rose petals by hand to release the aromas and add to the sherbet. Serve with ice and twists of lemon or lime.

Aam ka sherbet (mango sherbet)

Metric	Imperial
3 ripe mangoes, halved	*3 ripe mangoes, halved*
1.2 litres water	*2 pints water*
pinch of salt	*pinch of salt*
juice of 1 lemon (optional)	*juice of 1 lemon (optional)*
25–50 g caster sugar (or to taste)	*1–2 oz caster sugar (or to taste)*
crushed ice (optional)	*crushed ice (optional)*

Preparation time: 15–20 minutes

Squeeze the mango pulp into a bowl and discard the skin and stone. Add the water and stir to mix thoroughly. Add the salt, lemon juice and sugar and stir well until dissolved. Serve either chilled or with crushed ice.

Variation:
If available unripe green mangoes can be used. These should be placed under a preheated grill until the pulp feels soft. The skin will split and cracks will appear. Allow to cool, then peel off the skin.

Phalon ka sherbet (mixed fruit sherbet)

Metric	Imperial
about 100 g caster sugar	*about 4 oz caster sugar*
300 ml water	*½ pint water*
juice of 2 lemons	*juice of 2 lemons*
1.2 litres lemonade	*2 pints lemonade*
1 banana, peeled and sliced	*1 banana, peeled and sliced*
1 orange, sliced and quartered	*1 orange, sliced and quartered*
1 apple, quartered and thinly sliced	*1 apple, quartered and thinly sliced*
1 pear, quartered and thinly sliced	*1 pear, quartered and thinly sliced*
2 rings fresh or canned pineapple, thinly sliced	*2 rings fresh or canned pineapple, thinly sliced*
8–10 firm strawberries, hulled and sliced	*8–10 firm strawberries, hulled and sliced*
few grapes, halved and pips removed	*few grapes, halved and pips removed*
mint leaves, chopped or crushed by hand	*mint leaves, chopped or crushed by hand*
grated rind of 1 lemon	*grated rind of 1 lemon*
85 ml gin or vodka (optional)	*3 fl oz gin or vodka (optional)*

Preparation time: 15–20 minutes

Dissolve the sugar in the water by stirring well. Add the lemon juice and lemonade. Add the fruit and stir gently. Add the mint, lemon rind and gin or vodka. Mix well and serve chilled or with crushed ice.
Serves 8–10

Masala angoor sherbet (spiced grape sherbet)

Metric	Imperial
175 g white seedless grapes	*6 oz white seedless grapes*
1 litre water	*1¾ pints water*
1 × 15 ml spoon lemon juice	*1 tablespoon lemon juice*
about 50 g caster sugar	*about 2 oz caster sugar*
pinch of salt	*pinch of salt*
freshly ground black pepper	*freshly ground black pepper*

Preparation time: 10–15 minutes

Liquidize or thoroughly crush the grapes with a potato masher. Add the water and strain. Add the lemon juice and stir in the sugar and salt until dissolved. Sprinkle with pepper to taste and serve with ice.

From the front, clockwise: Masala angoor sherbet; Nimbo pani; Aam ka sherbet; Thandai; Phalon ka sherbet

Nimki
(seasoned flour crisps)

Metric	Imperial
225 g plain flour	8 oz plain flour
1 × 5 ml spoon salt	1 teaspoon salt
1 × 5 ml spoon caster sugar	1 teaspoon caster sugar
1 × 5 ml spoon onion seeds	1 teaspoon onion seeds
15 g butter or ghee	½ oz butter or ghee
1 ripe banana, peeled and mashed	1 ripe banana, peeled and mashed
water to mix	water to mix
oil for deep frying	oil for deep frying

Preparation time: 15 minutes
Cooking time: 10 minutes

Nimki, or namak pare, are diamond-shaped snacks, which can be flavoured with various essences, vegetables or fruits. Nimkis can be stored in sealed jars for 1–2 months. When glazed with sugar caramel they become a sweet snack, called shakar para or gauja.

Sift the flour, salt and the sugar into a bowl, and add the onion seeds. Rub in the butter or ghee, add the banana and enough water to make a soft, smooth dough. Roll out very thinly to about 3 mm/⅛ inch thickness. Then cut the dough diagonally into strips both ways to make small diamond shapes, and prick with a fork.
Heat the oil in a pan and fry the shapes until golden brown and crisp. Drain on kitchen paper and allow the shapes to cool.

Variations:
To make savoury nimki add either freshly ground black pepper or chilli powder to taste, and omit the banana and sugar.
To make shakar para, or gauja, to serve as a sweet snack, reduce the salt to a pinch and proceed as for the main recipe, with or without the banana filling. Make a rich sugar syrup with 275 g/10 oz sugar and 500 ml/18 fl oz water. Dissolve the sugar in the water, increase the heat and boil until a drop of the syrup forms a hard ball in a cup of cold water, but before the syrup turns golden. Add the fried nimki to the pan and stir to coat with the sugar caramel. Serve hot or cold.

Aloo bonda
(spiced potato in batter)

Metric	Imperial
120 g baisen flour	4½ oz baisen flour
salt	salt
pinch of baking powder	pinch of baking powder
about 1 × 2.5 ml spoon chilli powder	about ½ teaspoon chilli powder
about 150 ml water	about ¼ pint water

Filling:	Filling:
450 g potatoes, boiled, peeled and cubed	1 lb potatoes, boiled, peeled and cubed
2 green chillis, seeded and very finely chopped (optional)	2 green chillis, seeded and very finely chopped (optional)
15 g fresh ginger root, peeled and chopped	½ oz fresh ginger root, peeled and chopped
1 small onion, peeled and finely chopped	1 small onion, peeled and finely chopped
2 sprigs of coriander leaves, chopped	2 sprigs of coriander leaves, chopped
salt	salt
freshly ground black pepper	freshly ground black pepper
1 × 15 ml spoon lemon juice	1 tablespoon lemon juice
oil for deep frying	oil for deep frying

Preparation time: 20 minutes
Cooking time: 15 minutes

Aloo bonda, or batata wada, are deep-fried fritters which are a speciality of Southern India and Gujrat in the north. This is a very popular dish for all occasions.

Sift the baisen flour, salt and baking powder into a bowl. Add the chilli powder and sufficient water to make a smooth batter. Beat well, then set aside.
To make the filling, mix together the potato, green chilli, ginger, onion, coriander leaves, salt and pepper. Stir in the lemon juice and mix thoroughly. Dip your hands in cold water, then divide the filling into about 20 small balls. Dip these in the batter.
Heat the oil in a pan until a drop of the batter rises quickly and turns crisp. Deep fry the balls a few at a time until golden brown. Serve hot or cold with tomato ketchup or a chutney.

Variation:
In place of the lemon juice use 3 × 5 ml spoons/3 teaspoons mango powder or 1 × 15 ml spoon/1 tablespoon extracted tamarind pulp.

From the left: Nimki, Aloo bonda, Samosas

Samosas (meat-stuffed pastries)

Preparation time: 45 minutes
Cooking time: 40 minutes

Metric
150 g plain flour
pinch of salt
1 × 1.25 ml spoon baking
   powder
25 g butter or ghee
water to mix

Imperial
5 oz plain flour
pinch of salt
¼ teaspoon baking
   powder
1 oz butter or ghee
water to mix

Filling:
15 g ghee or 1 × 15 ml
   spoon oil
1 onion, peeled and
   chopped
225 g lean meat, very finely
   minced
salt
freshly ground black pepper
1 green chilli, seeded and
   very finely chopped
2–3 sprigs of coriander
   leaves, chopped
juice of ½ lemon or
   2 × 5 ml spoons mango
   powder

Filling:
½ oz ghee or 1 tablespoon
   oil
1 onion, peeled and
   chopped
8 oz lean meat, very finely
   minced
salt
freshly ground black pepper
1 green chilli, seeded and
   very finely chopped
2–3 sprigs of coriander
   leaves, chopped
juice of ½ lemon or
   2 teaspoons mango
   powder

Flour paste:
2–3 × 5 ml spoons plain
   flour mixed with a little
   water

Flour paste:
2–3 teaspoons plain
   flour mixed with a little
   water

oil for deep frying

oil for deep frying

Sift the flour, salt and baking powder, and rub in the butter or ghee. Add enough water to make a soft smooth dough. Cover and set aside.

To make the filling, heat the ghee or oil in a saucepan and lightly fry the onion. Add the mince and salt and pepper. Add a little water and gently fry the mince for 10–12 minutes until dry, stirring occasionally. Add the green chilli, coriander and lemon juice or mango powder and mix well. Remove from the heat and allow to cool.

Meanwhile knead the dough well and divide into 16–18 even-sized balls. Using a little flour, roll out one portion into a 10–13 cm/4–5 inch round. Cut across the centre, then apply the flour paste down the straight edge and bring the two corners together to make a cone, gently pressing the pasted edges together to secure.

Fill the cone with the filling, apply flour paste to the open mouth of the cone and seal the shape. Prepare the remaining samosas similarly.

Heat the oil in a deep frying pan and gently deep fry the samosas, a few at a time, until golden brown. Drain on kitchen paper and serve hot or cold with tomato ketchup or a chutney.

Makes 16–18

Variations:
To make vegetable samosas substitute the following for lean mince: 450 g/1 lb potatoes, boiled, peeled and cubed or 450 g/1 lb mixed peas, diced carrots, green beans and potatoes. Add 1 × 5 ml spoon/1 teaspoon garam masala to the spices.

Minced chicken meat or fish may be substituted for lean minced meat.

Halim (spiced beef or lamb with wheat)

Metric	Imperial
225 g whole or broken wheat	8 oz whole or broken wheat
salt	salt

Spicy meat sauce:

Metric	Imperial
25 g butter or ghee	1 oz butter or ghee
225 g onions, peeled and chopped	8 oz onions, peeled and chopped
2–3 × 2.5 cm sticks cinnamon	2–3 × 1 inch sticks cinnamon
8–10 cloves	8–10 cloves
8–10 small green cardamoms	8–10 small green cardamoms
4 large cardamoms	4 large cardamoms
1–2 bay leaves	1–2 bay leaves
1 kg lean beef or lamb, diced	2 lb lean beef or lamb, diced
50 g fresh ginger root, ground to a paste	2 oz fresh ginger root, ground to a paste
7–8 garlic cloves, peeled and crushed	7–8 garlic cloves, peeled and crushed
2½ × 5 ml spoons ground cumin	2½ teaspoons ground cumin
about 1 × 5 ml spoon chilli powder	about 1 teaspoon chilli powder
1 × 5 ml spoon ground turmeric	1 teaspoon ground turmeric
150 ml plain unsweetened yogurt	¼ pint plain unsweetened yogurt
1.2 litres water	2 pints water

To serve:

Metric	Imperial
100 g butter, melted	4 oz butter, melted
freshly ground black pepper	freshly ground black pepper
25 g fresh ginger root, peeled and finely chopped	1 oz fresh ginger root, peeled and finely chopped
2 green chillis, seeded and very finely chopped	2 green chillis, seeded and very finely chopped
3–4 sprigs of coriander leaves, chopped	3–4 sprigs of coriander leaves, chopped
2 lemons, cut into wedges	2 lemons, cut into wedges
450 g onions, peeled, sliced and crisply fried	1 lb onions, peeled, sliced and crisply fried

From the left: Kabuli channa; Halim

Preparation time: 45 minutes, plus overnight soaking
Cooking time: 2–2¾ hours

Halim can be served at any mealtime and is ideally frozen as it does not lose its flavour.

If wheat in whole or broken form is not readily available from Asian stores or health food shops, a mixture of oats, barley and split chick pea (channa daal) in any proportions will give a good result.

Garam masala or chilli powder can be sprinkled on the finished dish to make it more spicy.

Wash the wheat thoroughly in cold water. Dry on kitchen paper and if using whole wheat crush it coarsely using a tea towel and a rolling pin. Leave the wheat to soak overnight in cold water.

Drain, then place the wheat in a saucepan with water to cover and a pinch of salt. Cook the wheat for 40–55 minutes until it is soft, and has the consistency of porridge, stirring occasionally to prevent sticking. Alternatively use a pressure cooker and cook for about 15 minutes. When cooked, drain and set aside.

To make the sauce, heat the butter or ghee in a large, preferably non-stick, saucepan and fry the chopped onion until golden brown. Add the cinnamon sticks, cloves, cardamoms and bay leaves, and continue frying for 15–20 seconds. Add the meat, ginger, garlic, cumin, chilli powder, turmeric and yogurt. Mix well and cover with a lid. Gently cook for about 20–30 minutes until the mixture is nearly dry.

Increase the heat and fry the mixture for 1–2 minutes, then add the water. Cover and simmer for about 20 minutes until the meat is tender.

Add the cooked wheat to the mixture, cover and cook for 40–50 minutes over a very gentle heat, stirring frequently. Add a little extra water if the mixture is becoming too thick.

Serve piping hot with the melted butter poured over and pepper to taste. Garnish with chopped ginger, chilli, coriander leaves, lemon wedges and fried onion.

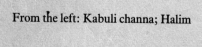

Kabuli channa or chhole (chick pea snack)

Metric
225 g chick peas
1 × 5 ml spoon bicarbonate of soda
40 g tamarind pods
2 × 5 ml spoons brown sugar
225 g potatoes, boiled, peeled and quartered
2 sprigs of coriander leaves, chopped
1–2 green chillis, seeded and very finely chopped
1 medium onion, peeled and chopped
salt
freshly ground black pepper
15 g cumin seeds, dry roasted and ground
juice of 1 lemon (optional)

Imperial
8 oz chick peas
1 teaspoon bicarbonate of soda
1½ oz tamarind pods
2 teaspoons brown sugar
8 oz potatoes, boiled, peeled and quartered
2 sprigs of coriander leaves, chopped
1–2 green chillis, seeded and very finely chopped
1 medium onion, peeled and chopped
salt
freshly ground black pepper
½ oz cumin seeds, dry roasted and ground
juice of 1 lemon (optional)

Preparation time: 45 minutes, plus overnight soaking
Cooking time: about 30 minutes

Wash the chick peas in cold water and soak them overnight with the bicarbonate of soda added to the water. Place the chick peas and their soaking liquid in a saucepan, adding enough fresh water to cover them and cook until soft in the centre. Alternatively use a pressure cooker and cook for about 10 minutes. Allow to cool. Then remove the lid and boil rapidly to dry off excess liquid.

Soak the tamarind pods in a teacup of hot water for 10–15 minutes and extract the pulp. Repeat this process to extract any remaining pulp. Stir the brown sugar thoroughly into the tamarind pulp and set aside. Mix together the chick peas, potatoes, coriander, chilli, onion, salt and pepper. Pour the tamarind mixture on top and stir well. Scatter over the ground cumin seeds, sprinkle with lemon juice and serve.

Variations:
To make a spicier version sprinkle the dish with garam masala and chilli powder.

Chopped or sliced fruit and vegetables can be mixed in with the other ingredients and this dish is called a chaat. The following are all suitable: banana, pear, apple, pineapple, peach, pawpaw, mango, guava, cucumber, tomato and radish.

FISH

In India, sea and freshwater fish are cooked in many different styles. As a peninsula with a large coastline, the coastal regions benefit from having an excellent choice of fish and the Bengalis and south Indians eat by far the largest amounts. The people of Bangladesh and the Bengalis use mustard oil to cook the fish.

The fish are frequently cooked with skin, bones and head intact, giving the dish full benefit of all the nutritional value, and this extracts the most flavour from the fish, too. If you are using frozen fish, cut or slice the fish before it is completely thawed so that the pieces retain their shape during preparation.

Chilli powder is used in these recipes. As it can vary in strength use it cautiously.

18

Tali machli
(dry spiced fish)

Metric	Imperial
about 1 × 5 ml spoon chilli powder	*about 1 teaspoon chilli powder*
1 × 5 ml spoon ground cumin	*1 teaspoon ground cumin*
1 × 5 ml spoon mango powder or 2 × 5 ml spoons lemon juice	*1 teaspoon mango powder or 2 teaspoons lemon juice*
salt	*salt*
freshly ground black pepper	*freshly ground black pepper*
4 × 175 g white fish fillets, rinsed and dried	*4 × 6 oz white fish fillets, rinsed and dried*
3 sprigs of coriander leaves, ground to a paste	*3 sprigs of coriander leaves, ground to a paste*
1 garlic clove, peeled and crushed	*1 garlic clove, peeled and crushed*
1 green chilli, seeded and crushed (optional)	*1 green chilli, seeded and crushed (optional)*
1 × 5 ml spoon garam masala	*1 teaspoon garam masala*
lemon juice (optional)	*lemon juice (optional)*
oil for frying	*oil for frying*
lime or lemon wedges	*lime or lemon wedges*

Preparation time: about 20 minutes
Cooking time: 40 minutes

This dish is just as delicious using any kind of fish, including shell fish. Instead of frying the fish it can be arranged in a baking tray, brushed with oil and either placed under a preheated grill or baked in a preheated oven 180°C, 350°F, Gas Mark 4 for 15–20 minutes.

Mix together the chilli powder, cumin, mango powder or lemon juice, salt and pepper. Sprinkle over the fish fillets.
Mix together the coriander, garlic and the crushed chilli. Rub this mixture well into the fish and sprinkle with garam masala. It may be necessary to use a little lemon juice to help the mixture adhere. Set aside for 7–10 minutes.
Heat a little oil and fry the fish, two at a time, for about 5 minutes on each side. Keep warm while frying the rest. Serve hot with lime or lemon wedges.

Bhoona prawn
(dry prawn curry)

Metric	Imperial
2 × 15 ml spoons oil	*2 tablespoons oil*
1 onion, peeled and diced	*1 onion, peeled and diced*
450 g peeled prawns	*1 lb peeled prawns*
3 garlic cloves, peeled and crushed	*3 garlic cloves, peeled and crushed*
1½ × 5 ml spoons garam masala powder	*1½ teaspoons garam masala powder*
about 1½ × 5 ml spoons chilli powder	*about 1½ teaspoons chilli powder*
1 × 2.5 ml spoon ground turmeric	*½ teaspoon ground turmeric*
salt	*salt*
200 ml water	*⅓ pint water*

To garnish:

1–2 green chillis, seeded and very finely chopped	*1–2 green chillis, seeded and very finely chopped*
2–3 sprigs of coriander leaves, chopped	*2–3 sprigs of coriander leaves, chopped*
lemon juice	*lemon juice*
1–2 tomatoes, sliced	*1–2 tomatoes, sliced*

Preparation time: 10–15 minutes
Cooking time: about 30 minutes

Heat the oil in a pan and gently fry the onion until tender. Add the prawns and continue frying until dry. Add the garlic, garam masala, chilli powder and turmeric, stir well and fry for 30 seconds. Add salt and the water. Cover and cook gently for 10–15 minutes until dry.
Garnish with the chopped chilli and coriander leaves, sprinkle with lemon juice to taste and arrange the tomato slices on top. Serve as a side dish with both rice and bread.

Variation:
Alternatively, mix together the chilli powder, turmeric, garam masala and garlic. Add the lemon juice, prawns and salt, then leave to marinate for 10–12 minutes. Fry the onion in the oil until just tender, then add the prawn mixture and water and continue frying for 10–12 minutes.

Tali machli; Bhoona prawn

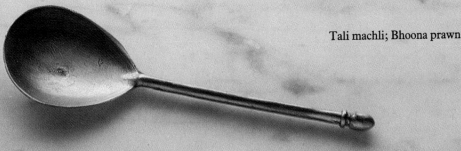

Machli ka salan (fish curry)

Metric	Imperial
40 g ghee or 3 × 15 ml spoons oil	1½ oz ghee or 3 tablespoons oil
2 onions, peeled and chopped	2 onions, peeled and chopped
25 g fresh ginger root, peeled and crushed	1 oz fresh ginger root, peeled and crushed
4–5 garlic cloves, peeled and crushed	4–5 garlic cloves, peeled and crushed
1 × 2.5 ml spoon ground turmeric	½ teaspoon ground turmeric
about 1 × 5 ml spoon chilli powder	about 1 teaspoon chilli powder
1 × 5 ml spoon ground cumin	1 teaspoon ground cumin
1 × 5 ml spoon ground coriander	1 teaspoon ground coriander
1 × 5 ml spoon garam masala powder	1 teaspoon garam masala powder
450 g white fish fillets, cut into 2.5 cm pieces	1 lb white fish fillets, cut into 1 inch pieces
1 × 400 g can tomatoes	1 × 14 oz can tomatoes
1 × 5 ml spoon salt	1 teaspoon salt
1 green chilli, halved and seeded	1 green chilli, halved and seeded

To garnish:

1 green pepper, cored, seeded and finely chopped	1 green pepper, cored, seeded and finely chopped
chopped coriander leaves	chopped coriander leaves

Preparation time: 15 minutes
Cooking time: about 20 minutes

Since frozen fish, which is the type most readily available here, flakes easily it is a good idea to add the fish towards the end of the cooking. Alternatively the fish can be fried separately and added to the sauce, or the dish can be cooked in a preheated oven at 160°C, 325°F, Gas Mark 3, for about 40 minutes. Cod, hake, halibut, coley, haddock, plaice or whiting are all suitable for this recipe.

Heat the ghee or oil in a large saucepan and fry the onion until light brown. Add the ginger, garlic, turmeric, chilli powder, cumin, coriander and garam masala. Fry for 15 seconds, then add the fish pieces and gently stir.
Add the tomatoes, salt and chilli. Cover and gently cook for 5–10 minutes or until the fish is tender. Remove from the heat and add the chopped green pepper and chopped coriander leaves. If preferred remove the chilli halves, then serve with bread or rice.

Tomatar jhinga (prawn curry with tomato)

Metric	Imperial
2–3 × 15 ml spoons oil	2–3 tablespoons oil
2 onions, peeled and cut into cubes	2 onions, peeled and cut into cubes
1 × 2.5 cm stick cinnamon	1 × 1 inch stick cinnamon
2 bay leaves	2 bay leaves
450 g peeled prawns, rinsed and drained	1 lb peeled prawns, rinsed and drained
5–6 garlic cloves, peeled and crushed	5–6 garlic cloves, peeled and crushed
25 g fresh ginger root, peeled and crushed, or 1 × 5 ml spoon ground ginger	1 oz fresh ginger root, peeled and crushed, or 1 teaspoon ground ginger
about 1 × 5 ml spoon chilli powder	about 1 teaspoon chilli powder
1½ × 5 ml spoons ground cumin	1½ teaspoons ground cumin
1 × 5 ml spoon ground coriander	1 teaspoon ground coriander
1 × 225 g can tomatoes or 3 tomatoes, skinned and chopped	1 × 8 oz can tomatoes or 3 tomatoes, skinned and chopped
1 × 5 ml spoon garam masala powder	1 teaspoon garam masala powder
salt	salt
100 g green pepper, cored, seeded and finely chopped	4 oz green pepper, cored, seeded and finely chopped

To garnish:

1–2 green chillis, seeded and very finely chopped	1–2 green chillis, seeded and very finely chopped
1–2 sprigs of coriander leaves, chopped	1–2 sprigs of coriander leaves, chopped

Preparation time: 15 minutes
Cooking time: 30–40 minutes

Heat the oil in a large saucepan and fry the onion until just tender. Add the cinnamon and the bay leaves, fry for 15 seconds, then add the prawns. Stir over the heat for 30 seconds.
Stir in the garlic, ginger, chilli, cumin and the coriander. Fry for 30 seconds, add the tomatoes and garam masala, and mix well. Add salt, cover and simmer gently for at least 15 minutes, until the prawns are cooked. Stir in a little water if necessary and add the green pepper a few minutes before removing from the heat.
Garnish with the chopped chillis and coriander leaves. Serve as a main dish with rice or bread.

From the left, clockwise: Prawn sukke; Tomatar jhinga; Machli ka salan

Prawn sukke (prawn curry with coconut)

Preparation time: 40 minutes
Cooking time: 1¼ hours

This particular curry comes from the Malabar coast of India and has a distinctly southern flavour, using coconut and tamarind in its ingredients.

Metric
25 g tamarind pods
450 g peeled prawns
50 g desiccated coconut
400 ml water
25 g creamed coconut
100 g frozen peas
4–5 curry leaves
1 green chilli, seeded and
  cut in half
40 g fresh ginger root,
  peeled and finely
  chopped, or about
  1 × 5 ml spoon ground
  ginger
2 tomatoes, skinned and
  diced
25 g ghee or 2 × 15 ml
  spoons oil
1 × 5 ml spoon fenugreek
  seeds
2 × 5 ml spoons ground
  coriander or coriander
  seeds
2 small whole red chillis
  (optional)
salt
1 large onion, peeled and
  chopped

Imperial
1 oz tamarind pods
1 lb peeled prawns
2 oz desiccated coconut
14 fl oz water
1 oz creamed coconut
4 oz frozen peas
4–5 curry leaves
1 green chilli, seeded and
  cut in half
1½ oz fresh ginger root,
  peeled and finely
  chopped, or about
  1 teaspoon ground
  ginger
2 tomatoes, skinned and
  diced
1 oz ghee or 2 tablespoons
  oil
1 teaspoon fenugreek
  seeds
2 teaspoons ground
  coriander or coriander
  seeds
2 small whole red chillis
  (optional)
salt
1 large onion, peeled and
  chopped

Soak the tamarind pods in a teacup of hot water for 10–15 minutes and extract the pulp.
Meanwhile rinse the prawns and drain well. Put the desiccated coconut in a bowl with 300 ml/½ pint of the water and leave for 10 minutes.
Blend the desiccated coconut with the soaking liquid and strain to get a creamy milk. Set the leftover pulp on one side. Place the creamy milk in a saucepan, add the creamed coconut, peas, curry leaves, green chilli, ginger, tomatoes and tamarind pulp, cover and allow to simmer for 10-15 minutes.
Heat 1 × 5 ml spoon/1 teaspoon of the ghee or oil in a separate pan and gently fry the fenugreek seeds, coriander and red chilli until the fenugreek turns light brown. Do not let the mixture burn and darken. Remove from the heat, allow to cool, then blend this mixture with the reserved coconut pulp and the remaining water to make a fine paste.
Heat a further 1 × 15 ml/1 tablespoon of the ghee or oil and fry the prawns until dry. Add the blended paste and gently fry for 5–6 minutes. Then transfer and stir this into the simmering coconut milk mixture and add salt. Simmer, covered, for 15–20 minutes.
Before serving fry the onion in the remaining ghee or oil then spoon it over the prawn curry. If preferred remove the chilli halves, and serve with boiled rice.

Madras mackerel curry

Preparation time: about 30 minutes, plus soaking
Cooking time: 50 minutes–1 hour

Metric
25 g tamarind pods
2 × 15 ml spoons cooking oil
1 onion, peeled and crushed or finely chopped
3 garlic cloves, peeled and crushed
about 1 × 5 ml spoon chilli powder
1 × 1.25 ml spoon ground turmeric
1½ × 5 ml spoons ground coriander
1 × 2.5 ml spoon cumin seeds, dry roasted and ground
1 × 2.5 ml spoon mustard seeds, dry roasted and ground
1 × 2.5 ml spoon fenugreek seeds, dry roasted and ground
15 g desiccated coconut
4–5 curry leaves
1 × 225 g can tomatoes
450 g mackerel, cleaned and cut into 5 cm pieces
1 green chilli, seeded and very finely chopped
salt

To garnish:
1 onion, peeled and chopped
2 × 15 ml spoons oil or 25 g ghee
1 × 5 ml spoon cumin seeds
chopped coriander leaves
piece of red chilli

Imperial
1 oz tamarind pods
2 tablespoons cooking oil
1 onion, peeled and crushed or finely chopped
3 garlic cloves, peeled and crushed
about 1 teaspoon chilli powder
¼ teaspoon ground turmeric
1½ teaspoons ground coriander
½ teaspoon cumin seeds, dry roasted and ground
½ teaspoon mustard seeds, dry roasted and ground
½ teaspoon fenugreek seeds, dry roasted and ground
½ oz desiccated coconut
4–5 curry leaves
1 × 8 oz can tomatoes
1 lb mackerel, cleaned and cut into 2 inch pieces
1 green chilli, seeded and very finely chopped
salt

To garnish:
1 onion, peeled and chopped
2 tablespoons oil or 1 oz ghee
1 teaspoon cumin seeds
chopped coriander leaves
piece of red chilli

Madras is the main city of Southern India and because of its closeness to the sea fish dishes are very popular. Southern Indian food tends to be more spicy than that in the north. This recipe uses unfilleted mackerel but for a less authentic version filleted fish may be substituted.

Soak the tamarind pods in a teacup of hot water for 10–15 minutes and extract the pulp. Repeat this process to extract any remaining pulp.
Heat the oil in a large saucepan and fry the onion until light brown. Add the garlic, chilli powder, turmeric, coriander, cumin, mustard seeds, fenugreek, coconut and curry leaves. Gently fry for 30 seconds. Add the tamarind pulp and the tomatoes, and simmer gently for 1 minute.
Carefully add the mackerel, then the chopped chilli and salt. Cover and cook for 30–40 minutes. If necessary add a little water.
To garnish, fry the chopped onion in the oil or ghee until light brown. Add the cumin seeds and as soon as they begin to crackle, pour the mixture over the fish curry. Sprinkle with the chopped coriander leaves, add a piece of chilli, and serve with plain boiled rice.

Madras mackerel curry; Masale vali machli;
Goan mackerel curry

Masale vali machli (dry fried herring)

Metric	**Imperial**
about 1 × 5 ml spoon chilli powder	about 1 teaspoon chilli powder
1½ × 5 ml spoons ground turmeric	1½ teaspoons ground turmeric
1 × 5 ml spoon ground ginger or ginger paste	1 teaspoon ground ginger or ginger paste
1 × 5 ml spoon garlic powder or garlic paste	1 teaspoon garlic powder or garlic paste
pinch of salt	pinch of salt
freshly ground black pepper	freshly ground black pepper
450 g herring fillets, cut into 5 cm pieces, with or without roes	1 lb herring fillets, cut into 2 inch pieces, with or without roes
oil for frying	oil for frying
1 lemon, sliced, to garnish	1 lemon, sliced, to garnish

Preparation time: about 20 minutes
Cooking time: 30 minutes

The herring is a bony, delicately flavoured fish and because of this it is generally fried rather than made into a curry.

Mix together the chilli powder, turmeric, ginger, garlic, salt and pepper. Rub this mixture into the fish pieces and set aside to marinate for 10–15 minutes. Heat a little oil and fry the fish pieces in two batches until golden brown. Remove and drain the fish. Serve hot, garnished with lemon slices.

Goan mackerel curry

Metric	**Imperial**
15 g tamarind pods	½ oz tamarind pods
2 × 15 ml spoons oil	2 tablespoons oil
1 small onion, peeled and chopped	1 small onion, peeled and chopped
about 1 × 5 ml spoon chilli powder	about 1 teaspoon chilli powder
1 × 2.5 ml spoon ground cumin	½ teaspoon ground cumin
2 × 5 ml spoons ground coriander	2 teaspoons ground coriander
100 g desiccated coconut	4 oz desiccated coconut
1 × 2.5 ml spoon ground turmeric	½ teaspoon ground turmeric
½ × 225 g can tomatoes, roughly chopped	½ × 8 oz can tomatoes, roughly chopped
5–6 curry leaves	5–6 curry leaves
1–2 green chillis, seeded and very finely chopped	1–2 green chillis, seeded and very finely chopped
salt	salt
7 fl oz water	⅓ pint water
450 g mackerel, cleaned and cut into 2.5 cm pieces	1 lb mackerel, cleaned and cut into 1 inch pieces

Preparation time: about 20 minutes, plus soaking
Cooking time: 30–40 minutes

Until the early sixties Goa was a Portuguese territory and the combination of Indian and Portuguese cooking styles have produced many famous dishes such as vindaloo and Goan curries, and certain pickles. Unfilleted fish is used in this curry for flavour and appearance, but filleted mackerel may be substituted.

Soak the tamarind pods in half a teacup of hot water for 10–15 minutes and extract the pulp. Repeat this process to extract any remaining pulp.
Heat the oil in a large saucepan and fry the onion until light brown. Add the chilli powder, cumin, coriander, coconut and turmeric. Fry for 30 seconds.
Stir in the tomatoes, tamarind pulp, curry leaves, chilli and salt. Add the water. Carefully stir in the mackerel, cover and gently simmer for 20–30 minutes until the fish is tender. Serve with plain boiled rice.

MEAT AND POULTRY

Lamb is the most popular meat eaten in India. Beef is avoided for religious reasons by the Hindus and it is also not of a particularly good quality. Cows are not farmed for beef, so only meat from old farm working animals is available. Pork is rarely eaten because it is forbidden by the Muslim religion and the climate increases the likelihood of tapeworms. Poultry is either roasted and served in tandoori style, or as a tikka dish, or simply made into curry or biryani.

As a general rule, all the tougher cuts of meat are cooked by a moist method such as stewing, braising, boiling or currying. Tender meat such as fillet, rump, loin and shoulder are good for dry heat cooking e.g. roasting, frying and grilling. For curries choose middle neck, shoulder, leg and scrag end, and it is common for the bones to be included, too. For biryani and pulao choose leg or shoulder, and for kebabs and keema use leg.

Chilli powder can vary in strength depending on the brand, so use it cautiously.

Pork vindaloo

Metric	Imperial
120 ml vinegar	4 fl oz vinegar
500 g lean pork, cubed	1 lb lean pork, cubed
1 large onion, peeled and roughly chopped	1 large onion, peeled and roughly chopped
1 × 5 ml spoon cumin seeds	1 teaspoon cumin seeds
2 × 5 ml spoons mustard seeds	2 teaspoons mustard seeds
5–6 garlic cloves, peeled and crushed	5–6 garlic cloves, peeled and crushed
15 g fresh ginger root, peeled, or 1 × 2.5 ml ground ginger	1/2 oz fresh ginger root, peeled, or 1/2 teaspoon ground ginger
4 cloves	4 cloves
1 × 2.5 cm stick cinnamon	1 × 1 inch stick cinnamon
6–8 peppercorns	6–8 peppercorns
40 g ghee or 3 × 15 ml spoons oil	1 1/2 oz ghee or 3 tablespoons oil
6–8 curry leaves	6–8 curry leaves
450 g tomatoes, skinned and chopped	1 lb tomatoes, skinned and chopped
1 × 2.5 ml spoon ground turmeric	1/2 teaspoon ground turmeric
salt	salt
2–3 sprigs of coriander leaves, chopped, to garnish	2–3 sprigs of coriander leaves, chopped, to garnish

Preparation time: 30 minutes, plus 15–20 minutes for marinating
Cooking time: about 1 hour

Although very little pork is consumed in India, this dish is a speciality of Goan cooking and vindaloo dishes always contain vinegar.

Blend 1 × 15 ml spoon/1 tablespoon of the vinegar with a little water and rinse the pork in this mixture. Drain and pat dry with kitchen paper. Grind the onion, cumin seeds, mustard seeds, garlic, ginger, cloves, cinnamon and peppercorns with a little of the remaining vinegar to a thick paste. In a large bowl or dish thoroughly mix the pork cubes with this paste, cover and set aside to marinate for 15–20 minutes.
Heat the ghee or oil and fry the curry leaves until golden brown. Add the marinated pork, tomatoes and turmeric, and keep stirring until the tomatoes are completely broken. Add any remaining vinegar and salt. Cover and simmer for about 40–50 minutes, until the pork is tender. A little water may be added during cooking if necessary, although the sauce should be fairly thick.
Garnish with coriander leaves and serve with rice.

Seekh kebabs (dry)

Metric	Imperial
1 green chilli, seeded and very finely chopped	1 green chilli, seeded and very finely chopped
15 g fresh ginger root, peeled, or 1 × 2.5 ml spoon ground ginger	1/2 oz fresh ginger root, peeled, or 1/2 teaspoon ground ginger
4–5 garlic cloves, peeled	4–5 garlic cloves, peeled
1–2 sprigs of coriander leaves, finely chopped	1–2 sprigs of coriander leaves, finely chopped
1 × 5 ml spoon cumin seeds	1 teaspoon cumin seeds
10 peppercorns	10 peppercorns
6 cloves	6 cloves
6 small cardamoms	6 small cardamoms
450 g lean minced beef or lamb	1 lb lean minced beef or lamb
1 small onion, peeled and very finely chopped	1 small onion, peeled and very finely chopped
about 1 × 2.5 ml spoon chilli powder	about 1/2 teaspoon chilli powder
salt	salt
1 egg (sizes 5, 6), beaten	1 egg (sizes 5, 6), beaten
a little oil	a little oil
1 lemon, sliced	1 lemon, sliced

Preparation time: 40 minutes
Cooking time: 4–6 minutes under the grill or 15–20 minutes in the oven

If you do not have many skewers, it may be necessary to make the kebabs in batches and keep them warm.

Grind the green chilli, ginger, garlic, coriander leaves, cumin, peppercorns, cloves and small cardamoms to a paste, adding a little water, if necessary. Mix the meat and onion together and stir in the spice paste, chilli powder and salt. Add enough beaten egg to make a firm consistency and mix thoroughly. Set the mixture aside for 2–3 minutes to allow the egg to bind it together.
Rub a skewer with a little oil. Shape some of the meat mixture around the skewer to a length of about 10 cm/ 4 inches. Repeat with other skewers.
Place the kebabs on a flameproof tray and put them under a preheated grill for 2–3 minutes on each side, brushing them with a little oil if necessary when turned. Alternatively arrange the kebabs on a wire stand in a baking tray and cook them in a preheated oven, 190°C, 375°F, Gas Mark 5, for 15–20 minutes, turning the kebabs to cook them evenly. The kebabs are also delicious barbecued on charcoal.
Serve with lemon slices.
Makes about 12

Pork vindaloo; Seekh kebabs

Roganjosh (rich lamb with almonds)

Metric	Imperial
50 g ghee or 4 × 15 ml spoons oil	2 oz ghee or 4 tablespoons oil
100 g onion, peeled and finely chopped	4 oz onion, peeled and finely chopped
5 small green cardamoms	5 small green cardamoms
1 × 2.5 ml spoon ground turmeric	½ teaspoon ground turmeric
about 1 × 5 ml spoon chilli powder	about 1 teaspoon chilli powder
1 × 5 ml spoon ground cumin	1 teaspoon ground cumin
1½ × 5 ml spoons paprika	1½ teaspoons paprika
1 × 5 ml spoon ground coriander	1 teaspoon ground coriander
150 ml plain unsweetened yogurt	¼ pint plain unsweetened yogurt
½ × 200 g can tomatoes, finely chopped	½ × 8 oz can tomatoes, finely chopped
1 small piece rattan jog (optional)	1 small piece rattan jog (optional)
500 g boned leg of lamb, cut into 2.5 cm cubes	1¼ lb boned leg of lamb, cut into 1 inch cubes
salt	salt

Masala:	Masala:
15 g fresh ginger root, peeled	½ oz fresh ginger root, peeled
6–7 garlic cloves, peeled	6–7 garlic cloves, peeled
1 blade of mace	1 blade of mace
1 × 1.25 ml spoon grated or ground nutmeg	¼ teaspoon grated or ground nutmeg
4 cloves	4 cloves
1 × 15 ml spoon poppy seeds, dry roasted (optional)	1 tablespoon poppy seeds, dry roasted (optional)
12 peppercorns	12 peppercorns
50 g almonds, blanched	2 oz almonds, blanched
2 large cardamoms	2 large cardamoms
pinch of saffron fronds (optional)	pinch of saffron fronds (optional)

chopped coriander leaves, to garnish	chopped coriander leaves, to garnish

Preparation time: 30 minutes
Cooking time: about 1 hour 10 minutes

This is a very rich preparation which is often made for special occasions such as weddings and feasts, and is sometimes embellished with edible beaten silver leaf called 'waraq'.

To make the masala, grind the ginger, garlic, mace, nutmeg, cloves, poppy seeds, peppercorns, almonds, large cardamoms, and saffron with a little water to make a fine paste.

Heat the ghee or oil in a pan and gently fry the onion until light brown. Add the small green cardamoms and stir in the paste of spices. Gently fry for 2 minutes, taking care not to burn the mixture. Add the turmeric, chilli powder, cumin, paprika and coriander and fry for a further 1–2 minutes. Stir in the yogurt and the chopped tomatoes. Add the rattan jog, lamb and salt, and stir well.

Cover and cook over a gentle heat for 40–50 minutes, sprinkling with a little water if necessary. Garnish with chopped coriander leaves. Serve as a main dish with pulao or fried rice and with bread.

Dum ka raan
(dry spiced roast lamb)

Metric
150 g fresh ginger root,
   peeled
8–10 garlic cloves, peeled
2 green chillis, seeded and
   roughly chopped
2 × 5 ml spoons cumin seeds
20 cloves
1 × 5 ml spoon peppercorns
3 large cardamoms
8 small green cardamoms
3–4 sprigs of coriander
   leaves
3 × 15 ml spoons lemon
   juice
1 × 15 ml spoon vinegar
150 ml plain unsweetened
   yogurt
about 1 × 2.5 ml spoon
   chilli powder
2 × 5 ml spoons ground
   coriander
2 × 5 ml spoons paprika
1 ¾ kg lean leg of lamb
salt
oil or fat for roasting
1 × 2.5 cm stick cinnamon
2 bay leaves

To garnish:
slices of lime
fresh mint
fried onion rings

Imperial
5 oz fresh ginger root,
   peeled
8–10 garlic cloves, peeled
2 green chillis, seeded and
   roughly chopped
2 teaspoons cumin seeds
20 cloves
1 teaspoon peppercorns
3 large cardamoms
8 small green cardamoms
3–4 sprigs of coriander
   leaves
3 tablespoons lemon
   juice
1 tablespoon vinegar
¼ pint plain unsweetened
   yogurt
about ½ teaspoon chilli
   powder
2 teaspoons ground
   coriander
2 teaspoons paprika
4–4¼ lb lean leg of lamb
salt
oil or fat for roasting
1 × 1 inch stick cinnamon
2 bay leaves

To garnish:
slices of lime
fresh mint
fried onion rings

Preparation time: 20 minutes, plus 40–50 minutes for
marinating
Cooking time: 1½–2 hours
Oven: 220°C, 425°F, Gas Mark 7
      200°C, 400°F, Gas Mark 6

In India a 'dum' is cooked by heat from above and
below, and this is achieved by covering the container
lid with hot cinders and then cooking on a wood or
charcoal fire.

Grind the ginger, garlic, green chillis, cumin seeds,
cloves, peppercorns, large and small cardamoms, and
coriander leaves with a little water to a paste. Mix this
paste with the lemon juice, vinegar and yogurt, and
add the chilli powder, coriander and paprika.
Make regular 2.5 cm/1 inch deep cuts across the meat
and sprinkle with salt. Rub in the spice mixture, cover
and leave for at least 40–50 minutes, turning the meat
from time to time and rubbing in any surplus spices.
To roast the meat, heat the oil or fat in a roasting tray.
Add the meat, the marinade, stick cinnamon and bay
leaves. Baste the meat with the marinade from time to
time and cook in a preheated oven for 30 minutes to
seal the juices. Reduce the oven temperature, cover
the meat with foil and continue cooking for 1–1½
hours, or until the meat is tender. Discard the
marinade and carve. Garnish with lime, mint and
onion rings.

Variation:
Alternatively pot roast the lamb. Heat 150–175 g/5–
6 oz fat or oil in a flameproof casserole or heavy
saucepan. Brown the meat quickly all over in the hot
fat. Add the marinade, cinnamon stick and bay leaves,
cover tightly and cook over a very low heat for about
1–1½ hours until tender. Baste and turn the lamb
over once or twice during cooking and sprinkle with a
little water if necessary.

Roganjosh; Dum ka raan

Korma gosht (meat curry)

Metric	Imperial
25 g ghee or 2 × 15 ml spoons oil	1 oz ghee or 2 tablespoons oil
1 onion, peeled and sliced	1 onion, peeled and sliced
2 bay leaves	2 bay leaves
1 × 2.5 cm stick cinnamon	1 × 1 inch stick cinnamon
about 8 peppercorns	about 8 peppercorns
8–10 cloves	8–10 cloves
4 small green cardamoms	4 small green cardamoms
2 large cardamoms	2 large cardamoms
450 g meat, e.g. lamb or stewing steak, cubed	1 lb meat, e.g. lamb or stewing steak, cubed
4–5 garlic cloves, peeled and crushed, or 1 × 5 ml spoon garlic powder	4–5 garlic cloves, peeled and crushed, or 1 teaspoon garlic powder
15 g fresh ginger root, peeled and crushed, or 1 × 5 ml spoon ground ginger	½ oz fresh ginger root, peeled and crushed, or 1 teaspoon ground ginger
about 25–50 g ground almonds (optional)	about 1–2 oz ground almonds (optional)
about 1 × 5 ml spoon chilli powder	about 1 teaspoon chilli powder
1 × 2.5 ml spoon ground turmeric	½ teaspoon ground turmeric
1½ × 5 ml spoons ground cumin	1½ teaspoons ground cumin
1½ × 5 ml spoons ground coriander	1½ teaspoons ground coriander
salt	salt
150 ml plain unsweetened yogurt	¼ pint plain unsweetened yogurt
300 ml water	½ pint water
10 g creamed coconut	¼ oz creamed coconut
chopped chilli or coriander leaves, to garnish	chopped chilli or coriander leaves, to garnish

Preparation time: 20 minutes
Cooking time: 1 hour

Heat the ghee or oil in a large pan and fry the onion until light brown. Add the bay leaves, cinnamon, peppercorns, cloves, small and large cardamoms, and continue frying for 30 seconds. Add the cubed meat and stir in the garlic, ginger, ground almonds, chilli powder, turmeric, cumin, coriander and salt. Fry for about 7 minutes until the meat is fairly dry and the oil or ghee separates and rises to the surface. Stir in the yogurt and gently fry to remove the moisture. Add the water, cover and cook over a gentle heat for 40–45 minutes, or until the meat is tender. Stir in the creamed coconut 5–10 minutes before removing from the heat. Garnish with coriander leaves, chilli, and edible silver leaf if available.

Pasanda (traditional curry)

Metric	Imperial
450 g lean meat, e.g. boned leg of lamb, cut into thin 2.5 cm strips	1 lb lean meat, e.g. boned leg of lamb, cut into thin 1 inch strips
150 ml plain unsweetened yogurt	¼ pint plain unsweetened yogurt
3–4 garlic cloves, peeled and crushed	3–4 garlic cloves, peeled and crushed
20 g fresh ginger root, peeled and crushed, or 1 × 5ml spoon ground ginger	¾ oz fresh ginger root, peeled and crushed, or 1 teaspoon ground ginger
1 × 5 ml spoon ground coriander	1 teaspoon ground coriander
1½ × 5 ml spoons ground cumin	1½ teaspoons ground cumin
15 g ground almonds or ground charoli nuts	½ oz ground almonds or ground charoli nuts
1 × 5 ml spoon garam masala powder	1 teaspoon garam masala powder
salt	salt
25–40 g ghee or 2–3 × 15 ml spoons oil	1–1½ oz ghee or 2–3 tablespoons oil
225 g onion, peeled and finely chopped	8 oz onion, peeled and finely chopped
120 ml water (optional)	4 fl oz water (optional)
3–4 green chillis, halved and seeded, or 1 × 5 ml spoon chilli powder	3–4 green chillis, halved and seeded, or 1 teaspoon chilli powder
lemon juice	lemon juice

To garnish:	To garnish:
chopped coriander leaves	chopped coriander leaves
flaked almonds	flaked almonds

Preparation time: 15 minutes, plus 1 hour for marinating
Cooking time: 1 hour 15 minutes

Charoli nuts are available from Asian food stores.

Put the meat, yogurt, garlic, ginger, coriander, cumin, almonds or charoli nuts, garam masala and a pinch of salt in a large bowl. Mix together well, cover and leave to marinate for 1 hour.
Heat the ghee or oil in a large frying pan and fry the onion until light brown. Add the marinated meat and fry until well browned. Cover and cook over a gentle heat for 40–45 minutes until the meat is tender. If the mixture becomes too dry before the meat is cooked add the water. Add the chilli halves, or chilli powder, and continue cooking for 5–8 minutes.
Sprinkle with lemon juice and garnish with coriander leaves and almonds. Serve with pulao rice and bread.

Chops masale vale (dry spiced lamb chops)

Metric
8 chump or loin lamb chops
about 1 × 2.5 ml spoon
  chilli powder
2 × 5 ml spoons ground
  ginger
2 × 5 ml spoons garlic
  powder
freshly ground black pepper
salt
150 ml plain unsweetened
  yogurt
about 1 × 15 ml spoon oil

Imperial
8 chump or loin lamb chops
about ½ teaspoon chilli
  powder
2 teaspoons ground
  ginger
2 teaspoons garlic
  powder
freshly ground black pepper
salt
¼ pint plain unsweetened
  yogurt
about 1 tablespoon oil

To garnish:
fried onion rings
wedges of lemon or lime

To garnish:
fried onion rings
wedges of lemon or lime

Preparation time: 10 minutes, plus 1–2 hours for marinating
Cooking time: about 15 minutes

Put the chops in a large bowl or dish and sprinkle over the chilli powder, ginger, garlic powder, pepper and salt. Add the yogurt, mix well, cover and leave to marinate for 1–2 hours.

Pour the oil on to the marinated chops and mix again thoroughly. Lift the chops out and place them under a preheated grill for 4–6 minutes on each side. Serve hot, garnished with lemon or lime and onion rings.

Variation:
Instead of grilling the chops, heat 1 × 15 ml spoon/1 tablespoon oil in a large pan and fry 1 chopped onion until tender. Add the marinated meat and any surplus marinade, cover and cook gently for 40–50 minutes, until the mixture is dry and the chops are cooked.

From the left: Korma gosht; Pasanda; Chops masale vale

Tomatar gosht (meat with tomatoes)

Metric
50 g ghee or 4 × 15 ml spoons oil
1 onion, peeled and chopped
25 g fresh ginger root, peeled and crushed
4–5 garlic cloves, peeled and crushed
1 × 2.5 ml spoon ground turmeric
1 × 5 ml spoon ground coriander
1½ × 5 ml spoons ground cumin
450 g braising steak or leg of lamb, cut into cubes
salt
1–2 green chillis, seeded and very finely chopped, or 1 × 5 ml spoon chilli powder
1 × 400 g can tomatoes
2–3 sprigs of coriander leaves, chopped

Imperial
2 oz ghee or 4 tablespoons oil
1 onion, peeled and chopped
1 oz fresh ginger root, peeled and crushed
4–5 garlic cloves, peeled and crushed
½ teaspoon ground turmeric
1 teaspoon ground coriander
1½ teaspoons ground cumin
1 lb braising steak or leg of lamb, cut into cubes
salt
1–2 green chillis, seeded and very finely chopped, or 1 teaspoon chilli powder
1 × 14 oz can tomatoes
2–3 sprigs of coriander leaves, chopped

Preparation time: 20 minutes
Cooking time: 1 hour 10 minutes

Heat the ghee or oil in a pan and fry the onion until light brown. Add the ginger, garlic, turmeric, coriander, cumin, the meat and salt. Mix together well, then cover and cook over a gentle heat for 10–12 minutes. Add the chillis, or chilli powder, the tomatoes and coriander leaves. Cover and cook for a further 50 minutes. Serve with chappatis, nan or parathas.

Goan meat curry

Metric
50 g ghee or 4 × 15 ml spoons oil
1 onion, peeled and chopped
5 small garlic cloves, peeled and chopped
450 g lean lamb or beef, cut into small pieces
5 garlic cloves, peeled and ground to a paste
25 g fresh ginger root, peeled and ground to a paste
3 green chillis, seeded and very finely chopped
1 × 2.5 ml spoon ground turmeric
2 × 5 ml spoons aniseed powder
salt
40 g creamed coconut
about 250 ml water
2–3 sprigs of coriander leaves, chopped

Imperial
2 oz ghee or 4 tablespoons oil
1 onion, peeled and chopped
5 small garlic cloves, peeled and chopped
1 lb lean lamb or beef, cut into small pieces
5 garlic cloves, peeled and ground to a paste
1 oz fresh ginger root, peeled and ground to a paste
3 green chillis, seeded and very finely chopped
½ teaspoon ground turmeric
2 teaspoons aniseed powder
salt
1½ oz creamed coconut
about 8 fl oz water
2–3 sprigs of coriander leaves, chopped

Preparation time: 30 minutes
Cooking time: about 1 hour

Heat the ghee or oil in a large pan and fry the onion and chopped garlic until the onion is light brown. Add the meat, the garlic and ginger paste, chopped chillis, turmeric, and mix well. Fry for 6–7 minutes until the meat is dry. Sprinkle on the aniseed powder, add salt, then stir in the creamed coconut. Fry for 1–2 minutes. Add the water and coriander leaves.
Cover and gently cook for 30–40 minutes, or until the meat is tender. Serve with slices of lemon and rice.

Meat Madras

Preparation time: 20 minutes
Cooking time: about 1 hour

Metric
50 g ghee or 4 × 15 ml
  spoons oil
1 small onion, peeled and
  chopped
450 g lean lamb or beef, cut
  into cubes
150–175 ml water
1 × 15 ml spoon coriander
  seeds
10 peppercorns
1 × 2 cm stick cinnamon
3 cloves
1 × 2.5 ml spoon chilli
  powder
1 medium onion, peeled
  and chopped
100 g fresh coconut, grated,
  or 65 g desiccated
  coconut
5–6 curry leaves
1 × 2.5 ml spoon ground
  turmeric
salt

Imperial
2 oz ghee or 4 tablespoons
  oil
1 small onion, peeled and
  chopped
1 lb lean lamb or beef, cut
  into cubes
5–6 fl oz water
1 tablespoon coriander
  seeds
10 peppercorns
1 × ¾ inch stick cinnamon
3 cloves
½ teaspoon chilli
  powder
1 medium onion, peeled
  and chopped
4 oz fresh coconut, grated,
  or 2½ oz desiccated
  coconut
5–6 curry leaves
½ teaspoon ground
  turmeric
salt

Madras is the main city of Southern India and is famous for many unique dishes, the special flavour of which is achieved with coconut and curry leaves.

Heat 40 g/1½ oz of the ghee or 3 × 15 ml spoons/3 tablespoons of the oil in a large pan and fry the small onion until light brown. Add the meat and water, cover and cook gently for 20–25 minutes until the meat is fairly tender. Remove from the heat, and stir until the softened onion is thoroughly incorporated.
In a separate pan, dry roast the coriander, peppercorns, stick cinnamon, cloves and chilli powder over a gentle heat for a few seconds, without letting them burn. Allow to cool and grind to a fine powder.
Heat the remaining oil or ghee and fry the medium onion until light brown. Add the coconut and curry leaves and cook for ½ minute, then add the turmeric, ground spices, salt and the cooked meat mixture. Cook for about 20 minutes until the meat is tender and the sauce has thickened, adding a little extra water if the mixture becomes too dry.
Serve as a main dish with pulao rice or parathas.

From the left: Nan; Goan meat curry;
Tomatar gosht; Meat Madras

Boti kebabs; Chops mirchwala; Shami kebabs

Chops mirchwala (pork chops in chilli sauce)

Preparation time: 25 minutes, plus 30–40 minutes or overnight marinating
Cooking time: 40–45 minutes
Oven: 180°C, 350°F, Gas Mark 4

Metric
8 garlic cloves, peeled, or 2 × 5 ml spoons garlic powder
15 g fresh ginger root, peeled, or 2 × 5 ml spoons ground ginger
1 × 15 ml spoon vinegar
about 1½ × 5 ml spoons chilli powder
8 pork chops, trimmed of excess fat
salt
a little oil

Imperial
8 garlic cloves, peeled, or 2 teaspoons garlic powder
½ oz fresh ginger root, peeled, or 2 teaspoons ground ginger
1 tablespoon vinegar
about 1½ teaspoons chilli powder
8 pork chops, trimmed of excess fat
salt
a little oil

Grind the garlic, ginger and the vinegar to make a thick paste. Add the chilli powder, mix well and rub this mixture over the chops. Cover and set aside for 30–40 minutes or leave overnight in a refrigerator. Sprinkle the chops with salt, brush them with oil, then place them in a casserole dish. Cover and cook in a preheated oven for 40–45 minutes, turning the chops a few times, until well cooked.

Boti kebabs (dry)

Metric	Imperial
25 g fresh ginger root, peeled and ground to a paste, or 2 × 5 ml spoons ground ginger	*1 oz fresh ginger root, peeled and ground to a paste, or 2 teaspoons ground ginger*
1 × 5 ml spoon garlic powder or garlic paste	*1 teaspoon garlic powder or garlic paste*
450 g boned leg or shoulder of lamb, cut into thin 2.5 cm lengths	*1 lb boned leg or shoulder of lamb, cut into thin 1 inch lengths*
1½ × 5 ml spoons chilli powder	*1½ teaspoons chilli powder*
2 × 15 ml spoons vinegar	*2 tablespoons vinegar*
1 × 5 ml spoon freshly ground black pepper	*1 teaspoon freshly ground black pepper*
salt	*salt*
juice of 1 lemon	*juice of 1 lemon*
a little oil	*a little oil*

Preparation time: 20 minutes, plus marinating
Cooking time: 7–10 minutes

The word 'boti' means small pieces of meat. Although boti kebabs are best cooked in a charcoal oven called a tandoor or barbecued on charcoal they can be successfully cooked under the grill or in the oven. If you do not have many skewers it may be necessary to make the kebabs in batches and keep them warm.

In a large bowl or dish mix the ginger and garlic with the meat. Sprinkle with the chilli powder, vinegar, pepper and add salt. Mix well to coat the meat with all the spices. Add the lemon juice, cover and set aside for at least 15–20 minutes to marinate. For a better result leave to marinate for 3–4 hours or overnight.
Before cooking, stir the marinated ingredients again, then thread the pieces of meat on to skewers. Place the kebabs on a flameproof tray and put them under a preheated grill for about 4–5 minutes on each side, brushing them with a little oil occasionally.

Variation:

These kebabs may also be cooked in the oven. Arrange the kebabs on a wire stand in a baking tray and cook them in a preheated oven 180°C, 350°F, Gas Mark 4 for 15–20 minutes, turning the kebabs to cook evenly.

Shami kebabs (dry)

Metric	Imperial
450 g lean meat, cubed e.g. boned leg of lamb	*1 lb lean meat, cubed e.g. boned leg of lamb*
1 small onion, peeled and sliced	*1 small onion, peeled and sliced*
1 × 2.5 cm stick cinnamon	*1 × 1 inch stick cinnamon*
1 bay leaf	*1 bay leaf*
125 g chick peas	*5 oz chick peas*
1 egg (sizes 5, 6), beaten	*1 egg (sizes 5, 6), beaten*
2 × 5 ml spoons garam masala powder	*2 teaspoons garam masala powder*
1 × 15 ml spoon ground almonds or charoli nuts	*1 tablespoon ground almonds or charoli nuts*
1 × 5 ml spoon freshly ground black pepper	*1 teaspoon freshly ground black pepper*
salt	*salt*

Filling:	Filling:
½ small onion, peeled and finely chopped	*½ small onion, peeled and finely chopped*
10 g fresh ginger root, peeled and finely chopped	*¼ oz fresh ginger root, peeled and finely chopped*
1 sprig of coriander leaves, chopped	*1 sprig of coriander leaves, chopped*
1 green chilli, seeded and very finely chopped (optional)	*1 green chilli, seeded and very finely chopped (optional)*
2 × 5 ml spoons lemon juice or plain unsweetened yogurt	*2 teaspoons lemon juice or plain unsweetened yogurt*
oil for frying	*oil for frying*

Preparation time: 45 minutes
Cooking time: 1 hour 10 minutes

Put the meat in a large pan and cover with water. Add the sliced onion, stick cinnamon, bay leaf and chick peas, cover and simmer for about 50–60 minutes until dry and the meat is very tender. Remove the cinnamon stick and bay leaf.
Use an electric blender or mince the mixture to a sausage meat consistency. Add the egg, garam masala, nuts, pepper and salt. Mix well and set aside.
To make the filling, put the finely chopped onion, ginger, chopped coriander leaves, chilli, lemon juice or yogurt and a pinch of salt in a bowl and mix well. Take a small portion of the meat paste and make a hollow in the middle. Put about 1 × 1.25 ml spoon/¼ teaspoonful of the filling in the hollow and pat the meat paste into a round flat shape to enclose the filling. Continue to make the rest of the kebabs similarly.
Heat the oil in a frying pan and shallow fry the kebabs for 2–3 minutes on each side until golden brown.
Makes 10–12

Kofte ka salan (curried meatballs)

Metric
450 g lean minced meat
1 × 5 ml spoon garam
  masala powder
1 × 2.5 ml spoon ground
  ginger
1 × 2.5 ml spoon garlic
  powder
1 × 5 ml spoon ground
  cumin

Sauce:
25–40 g ghee or 2–
  3 × 15 ml spoons oil
1 onion, peeled and
  chopped
1 × 2.5 cm stick cinnamon
4 small green cardamoms
1 bay leaf
4 cloves
1 × 5 ml spoon ginger paste
  or ground ginger
1 × 5 ml spoon garlic paste
  or garlic powder
about 1 × 5 ml spoon chilli
  powder
1 × 5 ml spoon ground
  coriander
1 × 1.25 ml spoon ground
  turmeric
150 ml plain unsweetened
  yogurt
salt
about 600 ml water

Imperial
1 lb lean minced meat
1 teaspoon garam
  masala powder
½ teaspoon ground
  ginger
½ teaspoon garlic
  powder
1 teaspoon ground
  cumin

Sauce:
1–1½ oz ghee or 2–3
  tablespoons oil
1 onion, peeled and
  chopped
1 × 1 inch stick cinnamon
4 small green cardamoms
1 bay leaf
4 cloves
1 teaspoon ginger paste or
  ground ginger
1 teaspoon garlic paste or
  garlic powder
about 1 teaspoon chilli
  powder
1 teaspoon ground
  coriander
¼ teaspoon ground
  turmeric
¼ pint plain unsweetened
  yogurt
salt
about 1 pint water

Preparation time: 30 minutes
Cooking time: 1 hour–1 hour 10 minutes

Mix together the mince, the garam masala, ginger, garlic and cumin and set aside.
To make the sauce, heat the ghee or oil in a large pan and fry the onion until light brown. Add the cinnamon, cardamoms, bay leaf and cloves and fry for 1 minute. Remove from the heat and stir in the ginger and garlic pastes or powders, chilli powder, coriander and turmeric.
Return to the heat and gently fry for 30 seconds. Add the yogurt and salt. Cover and cook until the mixture is dry and the ghee or oil separates from the spice mixture and rises to the surface. Gradually stir in the water, cover and allow to simmer for 10–12 minutes. With the reserved meat mixture shape 16–20 small balls and slide them, one at a time, into the sauce. Cover and simmer gently for 30–40 minutes. The thickness and quantity of the gravy can be adjusted by adding more water or reducing the excess liquid.

Variation:
This recipe can be used as the basis for Nargisi kofta, which resembles Scotch eggs. Hard-boil 10–12 eggs (sizes 5, 6) and allow them to go cold. Use the meat mixture to coat the eggs and gently fry them in a little oil until the outside is lightly browned. Prepare the sauce as described and carefully slide the balls into the sauce and cook as before.

Kofte ka salan; Keema

Keema (dry mince curry)

Preparation time: 10 minutes
Cooking time: 30–40 minutes

Metric
25 g ghee or 2 × 15 ml
  spoons oil
1 onion, peeled and
  chopped
1 × 2.5 cm stick cinnamon
4 small green cardamoms
2 large cardamoms
1 bay leaf
450 g lean minced beef or
  lamb
1 × 1.25 ml spoon ground
  turmeric
about 1 × 5 ml spoon chilli
  powder
1 × 5 ml spoon ground
  coriander
1½ × 5 ml spoons ground
  cumin
150 ml plain unsweetened
  yogurt or 1 × 225 g can
  tomatoes or 4–5 fresh
  tomatoes, skinned and
  roughly chopped
100 g frozen peas (optional)
salt

To garnish:
chopped coriander leaves
1 green chilli, seeded and
  very finely chopped

Imperial
1 oz ghee or 2 tablespoons
  oil
1 onion, peeled and
  chopped
1 × 1 inch stick cinnamon
4 small green cardamoms
2 large cardamoms
1 bay leaf
1 lb lean minced beef or
  lamb
¼ teaspoon ground
  turmeric
about 1 teaspoon chilli
  powder
1 teaspoon ground
  coriander
1½ teaspoons ground
  cumin
¼ pint plain unsweetened
  yogurt or 1 × 8 oz can
  tomatoes or 4–5 fresh
  tomatoes, skinned and
  roughly chopped
4 oz frozen peas (optional)
salt

To garnish:
chopped coriander leaves
1 green chilli, seeded and
  very finely chopped

Popular as a breakfast dish with parathas, keema is also used to fill samosas and for biryani. It is usually cooked until dry.

Heat the ghee or oil in a large pan and fry the onion until light brown. Add the stick cinnamon, small and large cardamoms, and the bay leaf. Continue frying for 1 minute.

Add the minced beef or lamb and sprinkle with the turmeric, chilli powder, coriander and cumin. Mix well and fry for 2–3 minutes to brown the meat, then add the yogurt or tomatoes, and salt. Cover and gently cook for about 10 minutes until the mince is dry. Uncover, add the peas, and continue cooking over a gentle heat for 10 minutes.

Serve garnished with coriander leaves and chilli.

Dam ke kebabs (dry baked kebabs)

Metric
450 g lean minced beef or lamb
1/2 large onion, peeled and finely chopped
2 × 5 ml spoons ginger paste
2 × 5 ml spoons garlic paste
about 1 × 5 ml spoon chilli powder
1 × 2.5 ml spoon ground turmeric
salt
oil for frying
1/2 large onion, peeled and sliced

Imperial
1 lb lean minced beef or lamb
1/2 large onion, peeled and finely chopped
2 teaspoons ginger paste
2 teaspoons garlic paste
about 1 teaspoon chilli powder
1/2 teaspoon ground turmeric
salt
oil for frying
1/2 large onion, peeled and sliced

To garnish:
green chillis, seeded and very finely chopped
chopped fresh ginger root
chopped coriander leaves
lemon wedges
raw onion rings

To garnish:
green chillis, seeded and very finely chopped
chopped fresh ginger root
chopped coriander leaves
lemon wedges
raw onion rings

Preparation time: 20 minutes, plus 2–3 hours for marinating
Cooking time: 50–55 minutes
Oven: 180°C, 350°F, Gas Mark 4

This dish is a speciality of the Hyderabad area, where it is made for special occasions.

In a large bowl or dish mix together the minced meat, finely chopped onion, ginger and garlic pastes, turmeric and salt. Mix well, then cover and leave for at least 2–3 hours in the refrigerator. If possible allow the mixture to marinate overnight.
Heat the oil and fry the sliced onion until golden brown. Remove with a slotted spoon, drain on kitchen paper and set aside. Mix the fried onion with the marinated ingredients and spread the mixture in a greased baking dish. Level the surface and brush the top with a little oil. Cook in a preheated oven for 40–45 minutes, by which time the mixture should be fairly dry.
Serve garnished with the chopped chillis, ginger, coriander leaves and lemon wedges. Raw onion rings can be arranged over the meat.

Variation:
Mix 85 ml/3 fl oz plain unsweetened yogurt and 2 × 5 ml spoons/2 teaspoons ground almonds with the minced meat at the same time as the spices.

Koorgi murgh (shredded chicken fry)

Metric
2 green chillis, seeded and roughly chopped
3 garlic cloves, peeled
50 g fresh ginger root, peeled
1 large Spanish onion, peeled and roughly chopped
1 × 15 ml spoon vinegar
1 × 1 1/2 kg chicken, or 4 chicken breasts, skinned, boned and shredded
3 × 5 ml spoons ground cumin
2 × 5 ml spoons freshly ground black pepper
salt
40 g ghee or 3 × 15 ml spoons oil
2 green peppers, cored, seeded and sliced
juice of 1 lemon

Imperial
2 green chillis, seeded and roughly chopped
3 garlic cloves, peeled
2 oz fresh ginger root, peeled
1 large Spanish onion, peeled and roughly chopped
1 tablespoon vinegar
1 × 3–3 1/2 lb chicken, or 4 chicken breasts, skinned, boned and shredded
3 teaspoons ground cumin
2 teaspoons freshly ground black pepper
salt
1 1/2 oz ghee or 3 tablespoons oil
2 green peppers, cored, seeded and sliced
juice of 1 lemon

Preparation time: about 50 minutes, plus 1 hour for marinating
Cooking time: 25–30 minutes

Boning and skinning a whole chicken takes time and patience, but it is often a cheaper alternative to buying portions.

Grind the green chillis, garlic, ginger, onion and vinegar to a paste. Place the shredded chicken and the paste in a large bowl or dish, mix thoroughly, then cover and set aside for 1 hour to marinate.
Add the cumin, pepper and salt to the marinated mixture and mix well. Heat the ghee or oil in a large pan, add the chicken, cover and fry over a gentle heat for 15–20 minutes.
Uncover the pan and add the sliced green pepper. Fry for a further 10 minutes or until the mixture is fairly dry and the chicken is cooked. Sprinkle with the lemon juice before serving.
Serve as a side dish with a main curry or simply with bread for a lighter meal.

From the front, clockwise: Dam ke kebabs; Murgh chaat; Koorgi murgh

Murgh chaat
(spicy chicken salad)

Metric	Imperial
about 175 g cooked chicken meat, shredded	about 6 oz cooked chicken meat, shredded
1–2 tomatoes, skinned and chopped	1–2 tomatoes, skinned and chopped
freshly ground black pepper	freshly ground black pepper
1 green chilli, seeded and very finely chopped	1 green chilli, seeded and very finely chopped
½ cucumber, chopped	½ cucumber, chopped
½ lettuce, coarsely shredded	½ lettuce, coarsely shredded
1 small onion, peeled and finely sliced	1 small onion, peeled and finely sliced
1 green pepper, cored, seeded and thinly sliced	1 green pepper, cored, seeded and thinly sliced
1–2 sprigs of coriander leaves, chopped	1–2 sprigs of coriander leaves, chopped
2 × 5 ml spoons cumin seeds	2 teaspoons cumin seeds
juice of 1 lemon	juice of 1 lemon
pinch of salt or black salt	pinch of salt or black salt

Preparation time: 30 minutes

The word chaat means to savour – a reflection of the tempting combination of salad ingredients, seasonings, and sometimes fruits, used in this dish.
This also makes a delicious light meal served on its own, in which case increase the quantities accordingly.

In a large bowl or dish, mix together the chicken and all the remaining ingredients. If possible leave the mixture for 30 minutes before serving. This allows the flavours to blend together.
Serve as a side dish or as a starter.

37

Murgh tomatar (tomato chicken curry)

Metric
40 g ghee or 3 × 15 ml spoons oil
1 onion, peeled and sliced
1 × 2.5 cm stick cinnamon
4 small green cardamoms
2 green chillis, halved and seeded
50 g fresh ginger root, peeled and finely sliced
6–7 garlic cloves, peeled and sliced
1 × 1½ kg chicken, cut into 8 pieces
2 × 5 ml spoons ground cumin
3–4 sprigs of coriander leaves, chopped
1 × 400 g can tomatoes

Imperial
1½ oz ghee or 3 tablespoons oil
1 onion, peeled and sliced
1 × 1 inch stick cinnamon
4 small green cardamoms
2 green chillis, halved and seeded
2 oz fresh ginger root, peeled and finely sliced
6–7 garlic cloves, peeled and sliced
1 × 3–3½ lb chicken, cut into 8 pieces
2 teaspoons ground cumin
3–4 sprigs of coriander leaves, chopped
1 × 14 oz can tomatoes

Preparation time: 30 minutes
Cooking time: 1 hour–1 hour 10 minutes

Heat the ghee or oil in a very large saucepan and fry the onion until light brown. Add the cinnamon, cardamoms, and green chillis and fry for 1 minute, then add the sliced ginger and garlic. Fry for 30 seconds, add the chicken portions and fry for a further 10–15 minutes.
Add the cumin and the coriander leaves and fry for 1–2 minutes, then stir in the tomatoes and salt. Cover and cook over a gentle heat for 30–35 minutes until the chicken is tender.
Serves 8

Goan chicken curry

Metric	Imperial
25 g tamarind pods	1 oz tamarind pods
25 g fresh ginger root, peeled	1 oz fresh ginger root, peeled
5–6 garlic cloves, peeled	5–6 garlic cloves, peeled
10 peppercorns	10 peppercorns
5 small green cardamoms	5 small green cardamoms
6 cloves	6 cloves
1 × 2.5 cm stick cinnamon	1 × 1 inch stick cinnamon
2 × 15 ml spoons vinegar	2 tablespoons vinegar
40 g ghee or 3 × 15 ml spoons oil	1½ oz ghee or 3 tablespoons oil
1 large onion, peeled and sliced	1 large onion, peeled and sliced
1 × 1½ kg chicken, cut into 8 pieces	1 × 3–3½ lb chicken, cut into 8 pieces
1 × 2.5 ml spoon ground turmeric	½ teaspoon ground turmeric
1–1½ × 5 ml spoons chilli powder	1–1½ teaspoons chilli powder
400 ml water	14 fl oz water
50 g creamed or desiccated coconut or fresh coconut, grated	2 oz creamed or desiccated coconut or fresh coconut, grated
salt	salt
1 × 5 ml spoon sugar (optional)	1 teaspoon sugar (optional)
few curry leaves (optional)	few curry leaves (optional)
slices of green pepper, to garnish	slices of green pepper, to garnish

Preparation time: about 45 minutes
Cooking time: 1 hour

Soak the tamarind pods in two teacups of hot water for 10–15 minutes and extract the pulp. Repeat this process to extract any remaining pulp.

Grind the ginger root, garlic, peppercorns, cardamoms, cloves and cinnamon with the vinegar to make a fine paste.

Heat the ghee or oil in a large pan and fry the onion until light brown. Add the chicken portions and fry for 5–6 minutes to lightly brown. Add the ground spices, turmeric and chilli powder, and fry for a further 1–2 minutes, then add the water and allow to simmer gently.

Add the coconut, the tamarind pulp, salt, sugar and curry leaves, and stir well. Cover and cook for about 45 minutes, or until the chicken is tender.

Garnish with green pepper and serve as a main dish with rice.

Serves 8

From the left, clockwise: Murgh tomatar; Murgh ka salan; Goan chicken curry

Murgh ka salan (chicken curry)

Metric	Imperial
40 g ghee or 3 × 15 ml spoons oil	1½ oz ghee or 3 tablespoons oil
1 large onion, peeled and chopped	1 large onion, peeled and chopped
1 × 2.5 cm stick cinnamon	1 × 1 inch stick cinnamon
6 cloves	6 cloves
1–2 bay leaves	1–2 bay leaves
4–6 small green cardamoms	4–6 small green cardamoms
2 × 5 ml spoons black cumin (optional)	2 teaspoons black cumin (optional)
1 × 1½ kg chicken, cut into 8 pieces	1 × 3–3½ lb chicken, cut into 8 pieces
25 g fresh ginger root, peeled and ground to a paste, or 2 × 5 ml spoons ground ginger	1 oz fresh ginger root, peeled and ground to a paste, or 2 teaspoons ground ginger
1½ × 5 ml spoons garlic powder	1½ teaspoons garlic powder
1–2 × 5 ml spoons chilli powder	1–2 teaspoons chilli powder
1 × 2.5 ml spoon ground turmeric	½ teaspoon ground turmeric
2 × 5 ml spoons ground cumin	2 teaspoons ground cumin
150 ml plain unsweetened yogurt	¼ pint plain unsweetened yogurt
salt	salt
450 ml water	¾ pint water

To garnish:	To garnish:
chopped coriander leaves	chopped coriander leaves
1–2 green chillis, halved and seeded	1–2 green chillis, halved and seeded

Preparation time: 40 minutes
Cooking time: about 1 hour 20 minutes

Heat the ghee or oil in a large pan and fry the onion until light brown. Stir in the cinnamon, cloves, bay leaves, cardamoms and black cumin, and fry for 1–2 minutes. Add the chicken and fry for 1–2 minutes.

Stir in the ginger, garlic, chilli powder, turmeric, cumin, fry for 1–2 minutes, then add the yogurt and salt. Cover and cook for about 10 minutes until the moisture has evaporated.

When the ghee or oil separates from the mixture and rises to the surface, stir in the water. Cover and cook gently for 30–40 minutes or until the chicken is tender. Taste and adjust the seasoning and add extra water or reduce the sauce, if necessary.

Garnish with chopped coriander and chilli. Serve as a main dish with rice and bread.

Serves 8

Tandoori chicken (dry)

Metric	Imperial
1 × 1½ kg chicken, cut into 8 pieces	1 × 3–3½ lb chicken, cut into 8 pieces
salt	salt
about 1 × 5 ml spoon chilli powder	about 1 teaspoon chilli powder
1 × 5 ml spoon freshly ground black pepper	1 teaspoon freshly ground black pepper
10 g fresh ginger root, peeled and ground to a paste, or 1½ × 5 ml spoons ground ginger	¼ oz fresh ginger root, peeled and ground to a paste, or 1½ teaspoons ground ginger
3 garlic cloves, peeled and ground to a paste	3 garlic cloves, peeled and ground to a paste
2 × 5 ml spoons paprika	2 teaspoons paprika
300 ml plain unsweetened yogurt	½ pint plain unsweetened yogurt
1 × 15 ml spoon lemon juice	1 tablespoon lemon juice
orange food colouring (optional)	orange food colouring (optional)
oil	oil

Preparation time: 20 minutes, plus 10–12 hours for marinating
Cooking time: 30 minutes

Tandoors are clay ovens used in India. All tandoori dishes are marinated and are cooked until dry.

With a sharp knife make regular slits through the skin and flesh of the chicken portions. Rub with salt. Mix together the chilli powder, pepper, ginger, garlic, paprika, yogurt, lemon juice and a few drops of orange food colouring. In a large bowl or dish pour this mixture over the chicken portions, cover and set aside to marinate for 10–12 hours. The longer it is left the better the result will be.
Place the chicken portions on a flameproof tray and put them under a preheated grill for about 15 minutes on each side, turning them regularly and brushing with oil occasionally.
Serve as a side dish with a fresh crisp salad.
Serves 8

Variation:
These chicken portions may also be cooked in the oven. Arrange them on a wire stand in a baking tray and cook them in a preheated oven 220°C, 425°F, Gas Mark 7 for 35–45 minutes, or until the juices run clear when pierced with a skewer, brushing the chicken with oil and turning them to brown all sides evenly.

Murgh makhanwalla (butter chicken)

Metric	Imperial
1 × 1½ kg chicken, cut into 8 pieces	1 × 3–3½ lb chicken, cut into 8 pieces
salt	salt
1 × 15 ml spoon lemon juice	1 tablespoon lemon juice
1 green chilli, seeded and roughly chopped	1 green chilli, seeded and roughly chopped
10 g fresh ginger root, peeled	¼ oz fresh ginger root, peeled
3 small garlic cloves, peeled	3 small garlic cloves, peeled
150 ml plain unsweetened yogurt	¼ pint plain unsweetened yogurt
2 × 5 ml spoons paprika	2 teaspoons paprika
1 × 1.25 ml spoon chilli powder	¼ teaspoon chilli powder
orange food colouring (optional)	orange food colouring (optional)
a little melted butter	a little melted butter
175 g unsalted butter	6 oz unsalted butter
150 ml soured cream	¼ pint soured cream

Preparation time: 30 minutes, plus 4–5 hours for marinating
Cooking time: 50–60 minutes
Oven: 220°C, 425°F, Gas Mark 7

With a sharp knife make regular slits through the skin and flesh of the chicken portions. Rub with salt, then sprinkle with the lemon juice.
Grind the green chilli, ginger and garlic to a fine paste. Mix this paste with the yogurt, paprika, chilli powder and a few drops of orange food colouring. Place the chicken portions and the spice mixture in a large bowl or dish, cover and set aside for 4–5 hours to marinate. Remove the chicken portions, place them in a greased baking tray and cook in a preheated oven for 45–50 minutes. Brush the portions with a little melted butter occasionally.
Melt the unsalted butter in a saucepan, add the remaining marinade and the soured cream. Gently heat, without boiling, for 5–6 minutes. Pour the sauce over the baked chicken and serve as a main dish with nan bread.
Serves 8

Variation:
Add 50 g/2 oz finely chopped cashew nuts or almonds to the simmering sauce.

From the front: Palak gosht;
Murgh makhanwalla; Tandoori chicken

Palak gosht (meat with spinach)

Metric	*Imperial*
1 kg fresh spinach, trimmed, washed thoroughly and chopped, or 2 × 225 g packets frozen leaf spinach, thawed and chopped	2 lb fresh spinach, trimmed, washed thoroughly and chopped, or 2 × 8 oz packets frozen leaf spinach, thawed and chopped
50 g ghee or 4 × 15 ml spoons oil	2 oz ghee or 4 tablespoons oil
1 small onion, peeled and sliced	1 small onion, peeled and sliced
40 g fresh ginger root, peeled and crushed, or 1 × 2.5 ml spoon ground ginger	1½ oz fresh ginger root, peeled and crushed, or ½ teaspoon ground ginger
5 garlic cloves, peeled and crushed	5 garlic cloves, peeled and crushed
1 × 5 ml spoon chilli powder	1 teaspoon chilli powder
1 × 5 ml spoon ground coriander	1 teaspoon ground coriander
1 × 5 ml spoon ground cumin	1 teaspoon ground cumin
4 fresh tomatoes, skinned and roughly chopped, or 1 × 225 g can tomatoes, roughly chopped	4 fresh tomatoes, skinned and roughly chopped, or 1 × 8 oz can tomatoes, roughly chopped
1 × 2.5 ml spoon ground turmeric	½ teaspoon ground turmeric
salt	salt
450 g boned leg or shoulder of lamb, cut into small cubes	1 lb boned leg or shoulder of lamb, cut into small cubes
200 ml water	⅓ pint water

Preparation time: 30 minutes
Cooking time: 50 minutes–1 hour 10 minutes

If using fresh spinach, place it in a saucepan with the water that clings to the leaves and cook for 10 minutes, then strain. Either sieve or blend the fresh or frozen spinach to make a purée and set aside.

Heat the ghee or oil in a large pan and fry the onion until light brown. Add the ginger, garlic, chilli powder, coriander and cumin and gently fry for 1–2 minutes. Add the tomatoes, turmeric and salt. Continue frying gently for 10–15 minutes, until the ghee or oil separates and rises to the surface. Add the meat and cook for 7 minutes, or until the meat is dry.

Add the water, cover and cook gently for 30–40 minutes. After about 15 minutes cooking time and when the sauce has been reduced by half, add the spinach purée. Stir well, cover and simmer gently.

VEGETABLES AND PULSES

Vegetables and pulses are an essential part of an Indian diet. Vegetable curries are either cooked dry, with the natural juices in the vegetables supplying the moisture, or with a little sauce, or made into a sort of purée (bhurta). A little water may be added to the dry-cooked vegetables to prevent them from sticking to the pan during cooking. Very little spice is used in cooking vegetables, and they should never be overcooked. Daals are made from many types of pulse. The most familiar in this country is the red split lentil, which does not need to be pre-soaked. Whichever pulse is used, however, the result is a delicious, thick, sauce-like accompaniment, which can be eaten with rice or bread for any meal.

Many dishes include chilli powder which can vary in strength and should be used cautiously.

Masoor ki daal; Sukhi tarkari

Sukhi tarkari (dry mixed vegetable curry)

Metric	Imperial
25–40 g ghee or 2–3 × 15 ml spoons oil	1–1½ oz ghee or 2–3 tablespoons oil
1 small onion, peeled and chopped, or 2 × 5 ml spoons cumin seeds	1 small onion, peeled and chopped, or 2 teaspoons cumin seeds
450 g diced mixed vegetables (e.g. potatoes, carrots, swede, peas, beans, cauliflower)	1 lb diced mixed vegetables (e.g. potatoes, carrots, swede, peas, beans, cauliflower)
about 1 × 5 ml spoon chilli powder	about 1 teaspoon chilli powder
2 × 5 ml spoons ground coriander	2 teaspoons ground coriander
1 × 2.5 ml spoon ground turmeric	½ teaspoon ground turmeric
salt	salt
2–3 tomatoes, skinned and chopped, or juice of 1 lemon	2–3 tomatoes, skinned and chopped, or juice of 1 lemon
300 ml water (optional)	½ pint water (optional)

Preparation time: 15 minutes
Cooking time: 20–25 minutes

Heat the ghee or oil in a pan and gently fry the onion until light brown. Alternatively fry the cumin seeds until they crackle. Add the diced vegetables, and stir in the chilli powder, coriander, turmeric and salt. Fry for 2–3 minutes.

Add either the chopped tomatoes or the lemon juice. Stir well and add only a little water if a dry vegetable curry is preferred. Cover and cook gently for 10–12 minutes until dry. For a moister curry stir in 300 ml/½ pint water before covering and simmer for 5–6 minutes, until the vegetables are tender.

Serve as a side dish, or as a main dish with rice or chappatis or nan.

Masoor ki daal (dry lentil curry)

Metric	Imperial
225 g red lentils, thoroughly washed	8 oz red lentils, thoroughly washed
450 ml water	¾ pint water
1 × 2.5 ml spoon ground turmeric	½ teaspoon ground turmeric
2 × 5 ml spoons ground coriander or 3 sprigs of coriander leaves, chopped	2 teaspoons ground coriander or 3 sprigs of coriander leaves, chopped
1 green chilli, halved and seeded (optional)	1 green chilli, halved and seeded (optional)
2–3 tomatoes, skinned and chopped, or 1 × 225 g can tomatoes, chopped	2–3 tomatoes, skinned and chopped, or 1 × 8 oz can tomatoes, chopped
salt	salt
6 curry leaves (optional)	6 curry leaves (optional)
50 g butter (preferably clarified)	2 oz butter (preferably clarified)
1 small onion, peeled and diced	1 small onion, peeled and diced

Preparation time: 15 minutes
Cooking time: 45–60 minutes

Various pulses, or daals as they are called in India, are generally cooked with similar spices. Therefore a variety of pulses can be substituted in this recipe to make various daals. The cooking times will vary and if preferred a pressure cooker can be used. Many pulses need to be soaked before cooking.

In a saucepan simmer the lentils in the water with the turmeric and coriander for 15–20 minutes until tender, or use a pressure cooker if preferred. With a potato masher, mash the lentil mixture. Stir in the green chilli, tomatoes, salt, and curry leaves. Cover and simmer gently for about 20–30 minutes. Remove from the heat and set aside.

Heat the butter in a pan and fry the chopped onion until light brown. Serve the daal with the onion mixture poured on top and with rice or bread.

Variation:

To make a sour daal (khatti daal), soak 25 g/1 oz tamarind pods, extract the pulp and add it to the last 2–3 minutes cooking time.

Sukhi bandhgobhi (dry cabbage curry)

Metric	Imperial
1 × 1.25 ml spoon fenugreek seeds	¼ teaspoon fenugreek seeds
1 × 5 ml spoon cumin seeds	1 teaspoon cumin seeds
1 × 2.5 ml spoon aniseed	½ teaspoon aniseed
1 × 2.5 ml spoon mustard seeds	½ teaspoon mustard seeds
1 × 2.5 ml spoon onion seeds	½ teaspoon onion seeds
25–40 g ghee or 2–3 × 15 ml spoons oil	1–1½ oz ghee or 2–3 tablespoons oil
2 medium potatoes, peeled and cut into chunks	2 medium potatoes, peeled and cut into chunks
1 bay leaf	1 bay leaf
450 g cabbage, chopped	1 lb cabbage, chopped
about 1 × 5 ml spoon chilli powder	about 1 teaspoon chilli powder
1 × 2.5 ml spoon ground turmeric	½ teaspoon ground turmeric
2 × 5 ml spoons ground coriander	2 teaspoons ground coriander
1 × 5 ml spoon sugar	1 teaspoon sugar
1 × 2.5 cm stick cinnamon or 1 × 2.5 ml spoon ground cinnamon	1 × 1 inch stick cinnamon or ½ teaspoon ground cinnamon
3 small green cardamoms	3 small green cardamoms
3 cloves	3 cloves
salt	salt

Preparation time: 10 minutes
Cooking time: 20–30 minutes

The mixture of seeds used in this dish is known as panch phoran and is a speciality of Bengal. It is used for many fish and vegetable dishes, and pickles.

In a small bowl mix together the fenugreek, cumin, aniseed, mustard and onion seeds. Heat the ghee or oil in a large pan and fry the potatoes for 4–5 minutes. Add the mixture of seeds and the bay leaf, and fry for a few seconds. Stir in the cabbage, chilli powder, turmeric, coriander and sugar. Cover and cook gently. Meanwhile, grind the cinnamon stick, cardamoms and cloves to a powder. Alternatively mix ground cinnamon into the powder. Sprinkle on to the cabbage, add salt and mix well. Cover and cook for a further 8–10 minutes or until the potatoes are tender.

Variations:
100 g/4 oz peas or cooked chick peas can be added 5 minutes before removing the curry from the heat.
Instead of the panch phoran mixture use 1 onion, peeled and chopped or 2 × 5 ml spoons/2 teaspoons cumin seeds.

Gobhi aloo (dry cauliflower curry)

Metric	Imperial
1 medium cauliflower	1 medium cauliflower
50 g ghee or 4 × 15 ml spoons oil	2 oz ghee or 4 tablespoons oil
1 medium onion, peeled and diced, or 2 × 5 ml spoons cumin seeds	1 medium onion, peeled and diced, or 2 teaspoons cumin seeds
2 medium potatoes, peeled and cut into chunks	2 medium potatoes, peeled and cut into chunks
about 1 × 5 ml spoon chilli powder	about 1 teaspoon chilli powder
1 × 2.5 ml spoon ground turmeric	½ teaspoon ground turmeric
2 × 5 ml spoons ground coriander	2 teaspoons ground coriander
salt	salt
2 × 5 ml spoons garam masala powder	2 teaspoons garam masala powder
2 × 5 ml spoons mango powder or juice of 1 lemon	2 teaspoons mango powder or juice of 1 lemon
water (optional)	water (optional)

Preparation time: 15 minutes
Cooking time: 25–30 minutes

Break the cauliflower into florets and cut into medium-sized pieces. Slice the remaining cauliflower stem after peeling away any tough skin. Discard the large leaves but retain a few of the tender smaller leaves. Wash the cauliflower pieces and leaves in cold water and drain thoroughly.
Heat the ghee or oil in a pan and fry the onion until light brown. Alternatively fry the cumin seeds until they crackle. Add the potatoes and fry for 2–3 minutes, then stir in the cauliflower pieces and leaves and continue frying for 5–6 minutes.
Stir in the chilli, turmeric, coriander, salt, garam masala and mango powder or lemon juice. Cover and cook gently for 10–15 minutes until the potatoes and cauliflower are tender and the mixture is dry. If necessary add a little water during cooking to prevent the mixture sticking. Avoid stirring the curry during cooking, otherwise the florets will disintegrate. Serve with chappatis.

Variation:
75 g/3 oz peas may be added 5 minutes before removing the curry from the heat.

From the front: Gobhi aloo; Sukhi bandhgobhi

Aloo Madras (dry spiced potato curry)

Metric
1 × 5 ml spoon cumin seeds
1 × 2.5 ml spoon fenugreek
    seeds
2 dried red chillis or
    1 × 5 ml spoon chilli
    powder
1 onion, peeled and chopped
25 g ghee or 2 × 15 ml
    spoons oil
8–10 curry leaves
1 × 5 ml spoon mustard
    seeds
450 g potatoes, boiled,
    peeled and cut into
    chunks
salt
1 × 2.5 ml spoon ground
    turmeric
1 × 15 ml spoon fresh or
    desiccated coconut

Imperial
1 teaspoon cumin seeds
1/2 teaspoon fenugreek
    seeds
2 dried red chillis or
    1 teaspoon chilli
    powder
1 onion, peeled and chopped
1 oz ghee or 2 tablespoons
    oil
8–10 curry leaves
1 teaspoon mustard
    seeds
1 lb potatoes, boiled,
    peeled and cut into
    chunks
salt
1/2 teaspoon ground
    turmeric
1 tablespoon fresh or
    desiccated coconut

Preparation time: 15 minutes
Cooking time: 30 minutes

In a frying pan dry roast the cumin, fenugreek and whole chillis or powder for 1 minute. Add the chopped onion and 2 × 5 ml spoons/2 teaspoons of the oil or ghee and continue frying for 1 minute. Grind the mixture with a little water to a fine paste.
Heat the remaining ghee or oil in a pan and add the curry leaves and mustard seeds. Fry for 30 seconds, then add the paste, the cooked potatoes, salt, turmeric and fresh or desiccated coconut. Add a little water, cover and cook gently for 3–4 minutes.

Dam aloo (dry potato curry)

Metric
450 g small potatoes,
    preferably new
1 medium onion, peeled
4 × 15 ml spoons oil
about 1 × 5 ml spoon chilli
    powder
1 × 2.5 ml spoon ground
    turmeric
25 g fresh ginger root,
    peeled and ground to a
    paste, or 1 × 5 ml spoon
    ground ginger
1 × 2.5 ml spoon sugar
salt
150 ml water
1 1/2 × 5 ml spoons garam
    masala powder
chopped coriander leaves,
    to garnish

Imperial
1 lb small potatoes,
    preferably new
1 medium onion, peeled
4 tablespoons oil
about 1 teaspoon chilli
    powder
1/2 teaspoon ground
    turmeric
1 oz fresh ginger root,
    peeled and ground to a
    paste, or 1 teaspoon
    ground ginger
1/2 teaspoon sugar
salt
1/4 pint water
1 1/2 teaspoons garam
    masala powder
chopped coriander leaves,
    to garnish

Preparation time: 20 minutes
Cooking time: about 30 minutes

Scrub or peel the potatoes and cut them into even-sized pieces. Boil the potatoes until just tender.
Grind the onion to a fine paste. Heat the oil in a pan and fry the onion paste until light brown. Stir in the chilli powder, turmeric, ginger, sugar and salt. Fry for 1–2 minutes without letting the mixture burn, then add the water. When the water begins to simmer, stir in the potatoes, cover and cook until the sauce has thickened. Sprinkle with the garam masala and remove from the heat. Garnish with coriander leaves before serving.

Aloo mattar (potato, pepper and pea curry)

Metric
40 g ghee or 3 × 15 ml spoons oil
1 small onion, peeled and chopped, or 1½ × 5 ml spoons cumin seeds
450 g potatoes, peeled and diced
about 1 × 5 ml spoon chilli powder
1 × 2.5 ml spoon ground turmeric
1½ × 5 ml spoons ground coriander
1 × 225 g can tomatoes
salt
100 g green peas
1 green pepper, cored, seeded and sliced
200 ml water
chopped coriander leaves, to garnish

Imperial
1½ oz ghee or 3 tablespoons oil
1 small onion, peeled and chopped, or 1½ teaspoons cumin seeds
1 lb potatoes, peeled and diced
about 1 teaspoon chilli powder
½ teaspoon ground turmeric
1½ teaspoons ground coriander
1 × 8 oz can tomatoes
salt
4 oz green peas
1 green pepper, cored, seeded and sliced
⅓ pint water
chopped coriander leaves, to garnish

Preparation time: 10 minutes
Cooking time: 15–20 minutes

Heat the ghee or oil in a large pan and gently fry the onion until light brown. Alternatively fry the cumin seeds until they crackle. Add the potatoes and fry for 3–4 minutes. Stir in the chilli powder, turmeric and coriander, and continue frying for 1–2 minutes. Add the tomatoes, salt, green peas, sliced peppers and stir well. Cover and cook gently for 1 minute, then stir in the water. Cook until the potatoes are tender. Garnish with chopped coriander leaves.

Palak aloo (dry spinach and potato)

Metric
40 g ghee or butter
225 g potatoes, peeled and cut into chunks
2 × 5 ml spoons garlic paste
2 × 5 ml spoons ginger paste
1 green chilli, halved and seeded
450 g fresh spinach, roughly chopped, or 225 g frozen chopped spinach
2–3 sprigs of coriander leaves, chopped
salt
50 g melted butter or ghee (optional)

Imperial
1½ oz ghee or butter
8 oz potatoes, peeled and cut into chunks
2 teaspoons garlic paste
2 teaspoons ginger paste
1 green chilli, halved and seeded
1 lb fresh spinach, roughly chopped, or 8 oz frozen chopped spinach
2–3 sprigs of coriander leaves, chopped
salt
2 oz melted butter or ghee (optional)

Preparation time: 10 minutes
Cooking time: 15–20 minutes

Heat the ghee or butter in a pan and fry the potatoes for 4–5 minutes. Add the garlic and ginger pastes and the chilli halves. Fry for 1–2 minutes. Stir in the spinach, coriander leaves and salt. Add a little water and continue frying for 10–15 minutes until the potatoes are tender and the spinach is dry. Serve with melted butter or ghee poured over the top.

Aloo Madras; Dam aloo; Aloo mattar; Palak aloo

Bean ki tarkari
(dry green bean curry)

Metric
50 g ghee or 4 × 15 ml
  spoons oil
2 red or green chillis
2 × 5 ml spoons urid daal,
  washed, soaked in cold
  water for 5 minutes and
  drained
6–7 curry leaves
175 g potatoes, peeled and
  diced
350 g sliced green beans
salt
1 × 15 ml spoon desiccated
  coconut

Imperial
2 oz ghee or 4 tablespoons
  oil
2 red or green chillis
2 teaspoons urid daal,
  washed, soaked in cold
  water for 5 minutes and
  drained
6–7 curry leaves
6 oz potatoes, peeled and
  diced
12 oz sliced green beans
salt
1 tablespoon desiccated
  coconut

Preparation time: 5 minutes
Cooking time: 20–30 minutes

Heat the ghee or oil in a pan and fry the whole chillis, the urid daal and curry leaves for a few minutes. Add the potatoes and continue frying for 5–6 minutes. Add the green beans, salt and the desiccated coconut. Cover and cook for 3–4 minutes. Stir and cook for about 5 minutes until the potatoes are tender.

Variations:
Fry 3–4 garlic cloves, peeled and crushed, with the urid daal.
Substitute 1 × 2.5 ml spoon/½ teaspoon each of chilli powder, ground coriander and ground turmeric for whole chillis, urid daal and curry leaves.

Toorai; Bean ki tarkari; Bhindi bhaji

Bhindi bhaji (dry okra curry)

Metric	Imperial
450 g okra	*1 lb okra*
40 g ghee or 3 × 15 ml spoons oil	*1½ oz ghee or 3 tablespoons oil*
1 medium onion, peeled and chopped	*1 medium onion, peeled and chopped*
225 g potatoes, peeled and cubed	*8 oz potatoes, peeled and cubed*
about 1 × 5 ml spoon chilli powder	*about 1 teaspoon chilli powder*
1½ × 5 ml spoons ground coriander	*1½ teaspoons ground coriander*
1 × 2.5 ml spoon ground turmeric	*½ teaspoon ground turmeric*
salt	*salt*

Preparation time: 15 minutes
Cooking time: 20–30 minutes

Wash, dry, top and tail the okra, then chop it into 1 cm/½ inch lengths. As okra has a gluey sap it should always be washed, dried and then cut. Heat the ghee or oil and fry the onion until tender. Add the potatoes and fry for 3–5 minutes.

Stir in the okra, chilli powder, coriander, turmeric, and salt. Cover and fry gently for 10–12 minutes until the potatoes are tender. If the mixture becomes too dry during cooking add 1 × 5 ml/1 teaspoon oil or ghee, or a little water. Serve with chappatis.

Toorai (courgette curry)

Metric	Imperial
25 g ghee or 1 × 15 ml spoon oil	*1 oz ghee or 1 tablespoon oil*
1 small onion, peeled and chopped, or 1 × 5 ml spoon cumin seeds	*1 small onion, peeled and chopped, or 1 teaspoon cumin seeds*
pinch of asafoetida (optional)	*pinch of asafoetida (optional)*
2 small potatoes, peeled and quartered	*2 small potatoes, peeled and quartered*
350 g courgettes, sliced	*12 oz courgettes, sliced*
about 1 × 2.5 ml spoon chilli powder	*about ½ teaspoon chilli powder*
1 × 2.5 ml spoon ground turmeric	*½ teaspoon ground turmeric*
1 × 5 ml spoon ground coriander	*1 teaspoon ground coriander*
salt	*salt*
1 × 2.5 ml spoon garam masala powder	*½ teaspoon garam masala powder*
chopped coriander leaves, to garnish	*chopped coriander leaves, to garnish*

Preparation time: 10 minutes
Cooking time: about 15 minutes

Heat the ghee or oil in a large pan and fry the onion until tender. Alternatively fry the cumin seeds and asafoetida until the seeds crackle. Add the potatoes and fry for 2–3 minutes. Stir in the courgettes, chilli powder, turmeric, coriander, and salt. Cover and cook gently for 8–10 minutes until the potatoes are tender. Sprinkle on the garam masala and garnish with chopped coriander leaves. Serve with chappatis.

Kaddu (pumpkin curry)

Metric	Imperial
450 g pumpkin	1 lb pumpkin
20 g tamarind pods	3/4 oz tamarind pods
40 g ghee or 3 × 15 ml spoons oil	1 1/2 oz ghee or 3 tablespoons oil
1 × 1.25 ml spoon cumin seeds	1/4 teaspoon cumin seeds
1 × 1.25 ml spoon mustard seeds	1/4 teaspoon mustard seeds
1 × 1.25 ml spoon fenugreek seeds	1/4 teaspoon fenugreek seeds
1 × 1.25 ml spoon onion seeds	1/4 teaspoon onion seeds
1 × 1.25 ml spoon aniseed	1/4 teaspoon aniseed
3 medium potatoes, peeled and cut into chunks	3 medium potatoes, peeled and cut into chunks
about 1 × 5 ml spoon chilli powder	about 1 teaspoon chilli powder
1 × 2.5 ml spoon ground turmeric	1/2 teaspoon ground turmeric
1 × 5 ml spoon ground coriander	1 teaspoon ground coriander
salt	salt
1 × 5 ml spoon sugar	1 teaspoon sugar

Preparation time: 25 minutes
Cooking time: about 30 minutes

Peel the pumpkin in alternate strips so as to keep the flesh intact during cooking, and cut into cubes. Wash and drain well.
Soak the tamarind pods in a teacup of hot water for 10–15 minutes and extract the pulp. Repeat the process to extract any remaining pulp.
Heat the ghee or oil in a pan and fry the cumin, mustard seeds, fenugreek, onion seeds and aniseed for 30 seconds, then add the potatoes and fry for 2–3 minutes. Add the pumpkin cubes, stir well and fry for 4–5 minutes.
Stir in the chilli, turmeric, coriander, salt and sugar, and continue frying for 5–6 minutes. Add the tamarind pulp, cover and cook until the potatoes are tender. Add 1 × 15 ml spoon/1 tablespoon water to the mixture during cooking if necessary.

Makkai (dry spiced sweetcorn)

Metric	Imperial
40 g ghee or 3 × 15 ml spoons oil	1 1/2 oz ghee or 3 tablespoons oil
1 small onion, peeled and chopped	1 small onion, peeled and chopped
1 medium potato, peeled and cubed	1 medium potato, peeled and cubed
2 green chillis, halved and seeded	2 green chillis, halved and seeded
5–6 curry leaves	5–6 curry leaves
175 g sweetcorn	6 oz sweetcorn
about 1 × 2.5 ml spoon chilli powder	about 1/2 teaspoon chilli powder
1 × 5 ml spoon ground coriander	1 teaspoon ground coriander
1 × 2.5 ml spoon ground turmeric	1/2 teaspoon ground turmeric
salt	salt
1 × 225 g can tomatoes	1 × 8 oz can tomatoes
2–3 sprigs of coriander leaves, chopped	2–3 sprigs of coriander leaves, chopped
1 × 5 ml spoon garam masala powder	1 teaspoon garam masala powder
lemon juice, to taste	lemon juice, to taste

Preparation time: 15 minutes
Cooking time: 20–30 minutes

Heat the ghee or oil in a pan and fry the onion until just tender. Add the potato and continue frying for 4–5 minutes. Add the chilli halves and curry leaves, fry for 1–2 minutes, then stir in the sweetcorn, chilli powder, coriander and turmeric and fry for 3–5 minutes until the mixture is dry.
Add salt and the tomatoes, cover and cook for 5–8 minutes, until the potatoes are tender and the sauce has thickened. Stir in the chopped coriander leaves, garam masala and lemon juice to taste.
Serve with chappatis or as a side dish or snack.

Variation:
Add slices of green pepper with the sweetcorn.

Shaljam ki tarkari (dry turnip curry)

Metric
450 g turnips, peeled
50 g ghee or 75 g butter
1 medium onion, peeled
  and sliced
1 green chilli, seeded and
  very finely chopped
1 × 5 ml spoon garam
  masala powder
salt
about 1 × 1.25 ml spoon
  sugar (optional)
juice of 1 lemon

Imperial
1 lb turnips, peeled
2 oz ghee or 3 oz butter
1 medium onion, peeled
  and sliced
1 green chilli, seeded and
  very finely chopped
1 teaspoon garam
  masala powder
salt
about 1/4 teaspoon sugar
  (optional)
juice of 1 lemon

Preparation time: 10 minutes
Cooking time: about 20 minutes

Slice the turnips into rounds and cook in 50 ml/2 fl oz boiling water until tender and dry.
Heat the ghee or butter in a pan and fry the onion until light brown. Add the chopped chilli, turnips, garam masala and salt. Taste and add sugar if liked. Cook for about 5 minutes.
Serve as a side dish sprinkled with lemon juice.

From the left, clockwise: Kaddu; Makkai; Shaljam ki tarkari

Daalcha (pulses with meat and vegetables)

**Preparation time: 50 minutes
Cooking time: 1½–1¾ hours**

In this recipe the meat should be left on the bone and chopped. Ideally ask your butcher to do this for you. It is important to use split chick peas rather than the whole variety which take longer to cook.

Soak the tamarind pods in 1½ teacups of hot water for 10–15 minutes and extract the pulp. Repeat this process to extract any remaining pulp.

Heat the ghee or oil in a large pan and fry the onion until light brown. Fry the stick cinnamon, garlic, ginger, and the meat for 4–5 minutes. Stir in the chilli powder, cumin, turmeric and tomatoes, and continue frying for a few minutes. Add the tamarind pulp, 750 ml/1¼ pints of the water, curry leaves and salt. Cover and gently simmer for 50–60 minutes until the meat is cooked.

Meanwhile, bring the remaining 450 ml/¾ pint water to the boil, add the chick peas and cook for 20–30 minutes until tender. Mash the mixture and set aside. When the meat is cooked stir in the chick pea daal, and the gourd, marrow, or courgette slices, and continue simmering until tender and the sauce is fairly thick. Add the chopped chilli and coriander leaves.

Variation:
Daalcha can be prepared without the meat.

From the left: Undey ka salan; Aloo gajjar; Daalcha

Metric
40 g tamarind pods
25–40 g ghee or 2–
    3 × 15 ml spoons oil
1 onion, peeled and diced
1 × 2.5 cm stick cinnamon
1 × 5 ml spoon garlic paste
    or garlic powder
1 × 5 ml spoon ginger paste
    or ground ginger.
350 g meat, e.g. breast of
    lamb, trimmed and
    chopped into pieces
about 1 × 5 ml spoon chilli
    powder
1 × 5 ml spoon ground
    cumin
1 × 2.5 ml spoon ground
    turmeric
2–3 tomatoes, skinned and
    sliced, or 1 × 225 g can
    tomatoes, chopped
1.2 litres water
8–10 curry leaves
salt
150 g split chick peas,
    thoroughly washed
200–225 g gourd or
    marrow, peeled, seeded
    and sliced, or courgettes,
    sliced
1 green chilli, seeded and
    very finely chopped
2–3 sprigs of coriander
    leaves, chopped

Imperial
1½ oz tamarind pods
1–1½ oz ghee or 2–3
    tablespoons oil
1 onion, peeled and diced
1 × 1 inch stick cinnamon
1 teaspoon garlic paste or
    garlic powder
1 teaspoon ginger paste or
    ground ginger
12 oz meat, e.g. breast of
    lamb, trimmed and
    chopped into pieces
about 1 teaspoon chilli
    powder
1 teaspoon ground
    cumin
½ teaspoon ground
    turmeric
2–3 tomatoes, skinned and
    sliced, or 1 × 8 oz can
    tomatoes, chopped
2 pints water
8–10 curry leaves
salt
5 oz split chick peas,
    thoroughly washed
7–8 oz gourd or
    marrow, peeled, seeded
    and sliced, or courgettes,
    sliced
1 green chilli, seeded and
    very finely chopped
2–3 sprigs of coriander
    leaves, chopped

Aloo gajjar (dry carrot curry)

Metric	Imperial
15–25 g ghee or 1– 2 × 15 ml spoons oil	½–1 oz ghee or 1–2 tablespoons oil
2 × 5 ml spoons cumin seeds	2 teaspoons cumin seeds
225 g carrots, peeled and diced	8 oz carrots, peeled and diced
225 g potatoes, peeled and diced	8 oz potatoes, peeled and diced
about 1 × 5 ml spoon chilli powder	about 1 teaspoon chilli powder
1 × 2.5 ml spoon ground turmeric	½ teaspoon ground turmeric
1 × 5 ml spoon ground coriander	1 teaspoon ground coriander
salt	salt
120 ml water	4 fl oz water

Preparation time: 10 minutes
Cooking time: 15–20 minutes

Heat the ghee or oil in a pan and fry the cumin seeds until they crackle. Add the carrots and potatoes, and continue frying for 5–6 minutes. Add the chilli powder, turmeric, coriander, salt and the water. Cover and cook for about 5–7 minutes until the carrots and potatoes are tender and the mixture is dry.

Undey ka salan (egg curry)

Metric	Imperial
25 g ghee or 2 × 15 ml spoons oil	1 oz ghee or 2 tablespoons oil
2 medium onions, peeled and chopped	2 medium onions, peeled and chopped
1 × 2.5 cm stick cinnamon	1 × 1 inch stick cinnamon
1 × 5 ml spoon garlic paste or garlic powder	1 teaspoon garlic paste or garlic powder
1 × 5 ml spoon ginger paste or ground ginger	1 teaspoon ginger paste or ground ginger
about 1 × 5 ml spoon chilli powder	about 1 teaspoon chilli powder
1 × 5 ml spoon ground cumin	1 teaspoon ground cumin
1½ × 5 ml spoons ground coriander	1½ teaspoons ground coriander
1 × 5 ml spoon garam masala powder	1 teaspoon garam masala powder
1 × 225 g can tomatoes, chopped	1 × 8 oz can tomatoes, chopped
salt	salt
300 ml water	½ pint water
2 × 5 ml spoons cornflour, blended with a little water (optional)	2 teaspoons cornflour, blended with a little water (optional)
8 hard-boiled eggs, shelled	8 hard-boiled eggs, shelled
coriander or celery leaves, to garnish	coriander or celery leaves, to garnish

Preparation time: 20 minutes
Cooking time: 50 minutes

Heat the ghee or oil in a pan and gently fry the onion. Add the stick cinnamon and stir for a few seconds. Stir in the garlic, ginger, chilli powder, cumin, coriander and garam masala, and continue frying gently for 30 seconds. Add the tomatoes and salt. Fry for about 5 minutes until the mixture is very thick. Stir in the water and if necessary add the cornflour to thicken. Carefully add the eggs, cover and simmer gently for 8–10 minutes. Garnish with coriander or celery leaves.

Baigan bhurta (spiced aubergine)

Metric	Imperial
450 g aubergines	1 lb aubergines
40 g ghee or 3 × 15 ml spoons oil	1½ oz ghee or 3 tablespoons oil
1 large onion, peeled and finely chopped	1 large onion, peeled and finely chopped
25 g fresh ginger root, peeled and finely chopped	1 oz fresh ginger root, peeled and finely chopped
3–4 garlic cloves, peeled and chopped	3–4 garlic cloves, peeled and chopped
about 1 × 5 ml spoon chilli powder	about 1 teaspoon chilli powder
1 × 2.5 ml spoon ground turmeric	½ teaspoon ground turmeric
3–4 sprigs of coriander leaves, chopped	3–4 sprigs of coriander leaves, chopped
1 green chilli, seeded and very finely chopped (optional)	1 green chilli, seeded and very finely chopped (optional)
salt	salt
4–5 fresh tomatoes, skinned and chopped, or 1 × 225 g can tomatoes	4–5 fresh tomatoes, skinned and chopped, or 1 × 8 oz can tomatoes

Preparation time: 10 minutes
Cooking time: 25–30 minutes

Spike the aubergines with a fork or skewer and place them under a preheated grill for about 15 minutes, turning the aubergine frequently until the flesh feels soft. Allow to cool. Scrape off the burnt skin with a knife. Chop the flesh.
Heat the ghee or oil in a pan and gently fry the onion until just tender. Add the chopped ginger and garlic. Fry for 1–2 minutes, then add the aubergine flesh. Stir in the chilli powder, turmeric, coriander leaves, chopped chilli, salt and the tomatoes. Fry for 10–15 minutes until dry. Serve with buttered chappatis.

Lehsun baigan (dry aubergine with garlic)

Metric	Imperial
40 g ghee or 3 × 15 ml spoons oil	1½ oz ghee or 3 tablespoons oil
2 medium potatoes, peeled and cut into chunks	2 medium potatoes, peeled and cut into chunks
4–5 garlic cloves, peeled and lightly crushed	4–5 garlic cloves, peeled and lightly crushed
450 g aubergines, cubed and put in salted water	1 lb aubergines, cubed and put in salted water
about 1 × 2.5 ml spoon chilli powder	about ½ teaspoon chilli powder
1 × 2.5 ml spoon ground turmeric	½ teaspoon ground turmeric
1½ × 5 ml spoons ground coriander	1½ teaspoons ground coriander
salt	salt

Preparation time: 15 minutes
Cooking time: about 20 minutes

Heat the ghee or oil in a pan and fry the potatoes for 5–6 minutes. Add the garlic and continue frying until the garlic is golden brown.
Drain and add the aubergine, stir in the chilli powder, turmeric, coriander and salt, and mix well. Add a little water, cover and cook gently for 8–10 minutes until the potato is tender. Do not stir too vigorously as the aubergine will disintegrate.
If preferred remove the garlic before serving.

Ghassey (dry chipped potatoes with garlic)

Metric
450 g potatoes, preferably
   new, scrubbed but not
   peeled
4–5 garlic cloves, peeled
   and lightly crushed
50 g ghee or 4 × 15 ml
   spoons oil
2 × 5 ml spoons urid daal
5–6 curry leaves
3 red or green chillis
salt

Imperial
1 lb potatoes, preferably
   new, scrubbed but not
   peeled
4–5 garlic cloves, peeled
   and lightly crushed
1½ oz ghee or 4 tablespoons
   oil
2 teaspoons urid daal
5–6 curry leaves
3 red or green chillis
salt

Preparation time: 10 minutes
Cooking time: 12–15 minutes

Cut the potatoes into very thin 2.5 cm/1 inch long chips. Wash thoroughly and drain well.
Heat the ghee or oil in a pan and gently fry the garlic until light brown. Add the urid daal and the curry leaves and gently fry for 30 seconds. Add the whole red or green chillis and fry for about 15 seconds.
Add the chipped potatoes and salt, and mix well. Cover and fry gently for 10–12 minutes until the chips are tender, turning them occasionally. If necessary a little water may be added during cooking. If preferred remove the garlic before serving.
Serve with a daal and rice, or parathas and rotis.

From the left: Baigan bhurta; Lehsun baigan; Ghassey

CHUTNEYS AND SALADS

Chutneys were very popular with the British Raj, who brought the idea back to Britain. They play an important part in an Indian meal and can be sweet or sour, mild or hot. There are no particular guidelines as to which chutney goes with which dish, they are all interchangeable according to one's own preference. They are served with snacks before a meal or with the main dishes.

There are two types, cooked or uncooked. The former keep very well in sealed jars like any other preserve, whereas the uncooked chutneys should be eaten within a day or two of making.

The term salad has been adopted by Indian terminology, after being introduced by the invaders and traders to ancient India. A dish of raw vegetables, with seasonings and fruit and nuts is a typical example. Salads are especially popular with tandoori and tikka dishes.

Raitas are yogurt-based vegetable or fruit salads. Their cool, refreshing flavours make a good, yet simple accompaniment to spiced foods.

Aam ki chutney; Pachari kosambari

Pachari kosambari (vegetable and nut salad)

Metric	Imperial
225–350 g bean-sprouts	8–10 oz bean-sprouts
100–150 g cabbage, shredded	4–5 oz cabbage, shredded
1 green chilli, seeded and very finely chopped	1 green chilli, seeded and very finely chopped
15–20 g fresh ginger root, peeled and finely chopped	1/2–3/4 oz fresh ginger root, peeled and finely chopped
2–3 sprigs of coriander leaves, chopped	2–3 sprigs of coriander leaves, chopped
1/2 cucumber, grated	1/2 cucumber, grated
salt	salt
lemon juice, to taste	lemon juice, to taste
1 eating apple or 1 ripe fresh mango	1 eating apple or 1 ripe fresh mango
50 g unsalted peanuts, roughly chopped	2 oz unsalted peanuts, roughly chopped
50 g unsalted cashew nuts, roughly chopped	2 oz unsalted cashew nuts, roughly chopped
1/2 coconut, flesh removed and grated	1/2 coconut, flesh removed and grated

Preparation time: 10–15 minutes

In a large bowl mix together the bean-sprouts, cabbage, chilli, ginger and coriander leaves. Discard any liquid and add the cucumber to the bean-sprout mixture. Sprinkle with salt and lemon juice to taste. Peel and grate the apple or mango and mix with the nuts and coconut. Add to the salad and toss well.

Aam ki chutney (mango chutney)

Metric
6 green mangoes
about 2 × 5 ml spoons
  salt
3–4 red chillis, roughly
  chopped, or 2 × 5 ml
  spoons chilli powder
300 ml malt vinegar
400 g sugar
25–40 g fresh ginger
  root, peeled and
  chopped
100 g mixed unsalted
  nuts and raisins,
  roughly chopped
  (optional)

Imperial
6 green mangoes
about 2 teaspoons
  salt
3–4 red chillis, roughly
  chopped, or 2 teaspoons
  chilli powder
½ pint malt vinegar
14 oz sugar
1–1½ oz fresh ginger
  root, peeled and
  chopped
4 oz mixed unsalted
  nuts and raisins,
  roughly chopped
  (optional)

Preparation time: 25 minutes, plus 30 minutes soaking
Cooking time: about 30 minutes

Almonds, cashew or pecan nuts are especially good for this chutney.

Peel the mangoes and grate the flesh into a bowl. Sprinkle with 2 × 5 ml spoons/2 teaspoons of the salt and set aside for 30 minutes.
Grind either the chillis or mix the chilli powder with a little of the vinegar to a fine paste. Place the remaining vinegar in a pan, add the sugar and gently simmer, stirring, until the sugar dissolves. Squeeze the grated mangoes with the back of a spoon to extract the juice, and discard. Add the mango flesh to the pan and gently simmer for a further 5–6 minutes. Add the ginger and the chilli paste and mix well. Cook for 10–12 minutes.
Taste and add a pinch of salt. Stir in the chopped nuts and raisins and cook for 4 minutes. Remove from the heat and allow to cool. Bottle in airtight jars with vinegar-proof tops.

Variations:
Add 2 × 5 ml spoons/2 teaspoons cumin seeds, dry roasted, 2 × 5 ml spoons/2 teaspoons ground coriander and 225 g/8 oz dessert or dried dates to the chutney during cooking.
Add 2–3 garlic cloves, peeled and crushed, at the same stage as the ginger.

Kakri raita (cucumber raita)

Metric	Imperial
250 ml plain unsweetened yogurt	8 fl oz plain unsweetened yogurt
½ cucumber, grated or sliced	½ cucumber, grated or sliced
salt	salt
1 × 5 ml spoon freshly ground black pepper	1 teaspoon freshly ground black pepper
1 green or red chilli, seeded and very finely chopped (optional)	1 green or red chilli, seeded and very finely chopped (optional)
1–2 sprigs of coriander leaves, chopped	1–2 sprigs of coriander leaves, chopped
a piece of chilli, to garnish	a piece of chilli, to garnish

Preparation time: 5–7 minutes

In a bowl beat the yogurt. Add the other ingredients, mix well and chill. Garnish the raita with a piece of chilli.

Serve as a side dish with roti and as an accompaniment to a main dish such as a biryani.

Baigan raita (aubergine raita)

Metric	Imperial
oil for deep frying	oil for deep frying
350 g aubergine, sliced into 3 mm rounds	12 oz aubergine, sliced into ⅛ inch rounds
300 ml plain unsweetened yogurt	½ pint plain unsweetened yogurt
salt	salt
2 × 5 ml spoons cumin seeds, dry roasted and coarsely ground	2 teaspoons cumin seeds, dry roasted and coarsely ground
1–2 × 5 ml spoons chilli powder	1–2 teaspoons chilli powder

Preparation time: 10 minutes
Cooking time: 15 minutes

Heat the oil in a deep frying pan and fry the aubergine slices until golden brown. Remove and drain well.

In a bowl beat together the yogurt and salt, then pour into a serving dish. Add the fried aubergine and sprinkle with ground cumin and chilli powder.

Variation:
Fry and mash the aubergine, and mix with the yogurt. Sprinkle with chopped chilli and coriander leaves.

Tarkari ka raita (mixed vegetable raita)

Metric	Imperial
300 ml plain unsweetened yogurt	½ pint plain unsweetened yogurt
1–2 × 5 ml spoons freshly ground black pepper or chilli powder	1–2 teaspoons freshly ground black pepper or chilli powder
salt	salt
¼ cucumber, diced	¼ cucumber, diced
1 small onion, peeled and diced	1 small onion, peeled and diced
1–2 potatoes, boiled, peeled and cubed	1–2 potatoes, boiled, peeled and cubed
2–3 tomatoes, chopped	2–3 tomatoes, chopped
100 g radishes, trimmed and sliced	4 oz radishes, trimmed and sliced
1–2 sticks celery, diced	1–2 sticks celery, diced
1 green chilli, seeded and very finely chopped (optional)	1 green chilli, seeded and very finely chopped (optional)
To Garnish:	**To garnish:**
1–2 sprigs of coriander leaves, chopped	1–2 sprigs of coriander leaves, chopped
slice of radish	slice of radish

Preparation time: 8–10 minutes

In a bowl beat the yogurt to a smooth consistency with the pepper or chilli powder and salt. Add the vegetables and mix well. Sprinkle on the green chilli and chill before serving.

Garnish with coriander leaves and a slice of radish.

Variations:
An eating apple, cut into cubes, or another fruit may be added.

A little lemon juice can be sprinkled on the raita before serving.

Use soured cream or French dressing or a Roquefort dressing instead of yogurt.

From the front, clockwise: Tarkari ka raita; Kakri raita; Baigan raita; Boondi raita

Boondi raita (traditional raita)

Preparation time: 10–15 minutes
Cooking time: about 20 minutes

Metric
50 g baisen flour
pinch of baking powder
4–5 × 15 ml spoons water
oil for deep frying

Imperial
2 oz baisen flour
pinch of baking powder
4–5 tablespoons water
oil for deep frying

Raita:
300 ml plain unsweetened
   yogurt
salt
freshly ground black pepper
1 × 5 ml spoon cumin seeds,
   dry roasted and coarsely
   ground

Raita:
½ pint plain unsweetened
   yogurt
salt
freshly ground black pepper
1 teaspoon cumin seeds, dry
   roasted and coarsely
   ground

To garnish:
1 green chilli, seeded and
   very finely chopped
1–2 sprigs of coriander
   leaves, chopped

To garnish:
1 green chilli, seeded and
   very finely chopped
1–2 sprigs of coriander
   leaves, chopped

Boondi are small fried balls and, if preferred, can be bought from Asian shops ready made. In this dish they are incorporated in a raita.

In a bowl sift the flour and baking powder. Gradually beat in enough water to make a thick batter.
Heat the oil in a deep frying pan. Pour a little of the batter on a ladle with holes and quickly shake the ladle over the top of the frying pan so that small drops of the batter fall in the oil. Fry for 3–4 minutes until crisp, then drain the boondi on kitchen paper. Leave to soften in a little cold water, while frying the remaining boondi. Gently squeeze the boondi to remove most of the water, place in a dish and set aside.
In a bowl beat together the yogurt, salt and pepper. Stir in the boondi. Sprinkle with the cumin, garnish with chopped chilli and coriander leaves, and chill before serving.
Serve with a main dish or with stuffed parathas.

59

Keley ki chutney (banana chutney)

Metric
50–75 g tamarind pods
2 × 15 ml spoons sugar
50 g raisins and
    sultanas
about 1 × 5 ml spoon
    chilli powder, dry
    roasted
15 g fresh ginger
    root, peeled and
    grated
pinch of salt
2–3 ripe bananas,
    peeled and sliced
1 × 5 ml spoon cumin
    seeds, dry roasted
    and ground
a little lemon juice
    or water (optional)

Imperial
2–3 oz tamarind pods
2 tablespoons sugar
2 oz raisins and
    sultanas
about 1 teaspoon
    chilli powder, dry
    roasted
1/2 oz fresh ginger
    root, peeled and
    grated
pinch of salt
2–3 ripe bananas,
    peeled and sliced
1 teaspoon cumin
    seeds, dry roasted
    and ground
a little lemon juice
    or water (optional)

Preparation time: 10 minutes

Soak the tamarind pods in two or three teacups of hot water for 10–15 minutes and extract the pulp. Repeat this process to extract any remaining pulp.
In a bowl mix together the tamarind pulp, sugar, raisins, sultanas and chilli powder, and stir until the sugar dissolves. Add the ginger, salt and banana. Sprinkle with the cumin powder. Add a little lemon juice or water to thin down the chutney if necessary.

Variations:
The bananas can be mashed instead of sliced.
225 g/8 oz dessert or dried dates may be added. Soak dried dates in warm water for 5–10 minutes before using. Remove the stones and slice the dates.

Sev ki chutney (apple chutney)

Metric	Imperial
1¼ kg cooking apples, peeled and cored	2½ lb cooking apples, peeled and cored
1 × 15 ml spoon salt	1 tablespoon salt
500 ml malt vinegar	18 fl oz malt vinegar
275 g soft brown sugar	10 oz soft brown sugar
100 g raisins	4 oz raisins
100 g sultanas	4 oz sultanas
1 × 2.5 ml spoon mustard seeds	½ teaspoon mustard seeds
25 g fresh ginger root, peeled and sliced	1 oz fresh ginger root, peeled and sliced
1–2 garlic cloves, peeled and chopped	1–2 garlic cloves, peeled and chopped
1 × 5 ml spoon chilli powder	1 teaspoon chilli powder

Preparation time: 15 minutes
Cooking time: about 20 minutes

Let this chutney mature for 4–5 weeks before using.

Slice the apples and lay them on a dish, and sprinkle with half of the salt. Cover and set aside.
Place half of the vinegar in a pan, add the sugar and stir over a low heat until the sugar is dissolved. Bring to the boil until a thick syrup is made. Allow to cool. Place the remaining vinegar in a pan, add the apples and simmer for 3–4 minutes until tender. Allow to cool then stir in the vinegar syrup, raisins, sultanas, mustard seeds, salt, chopped ginger, garlic and chilli powder. Bottle in airtight jars with vinegar-proof tops.

Keley ki chutney; Sev ki chutney; Phalon ka chaat

Phalon ka chaat (fruit savoury)

Metric	Imperial
2 eating apples, cored and sliced	2 eating apples, cored and sliced
2–3 bananas, peeled and sliced	2–3 bananas, peeled and sliced
1 pear, peeled and sliced	1 pear, peeled and sliced
1 orange, peeled, pith removed, seeded, segmented and cut in half	1 orange, peeled, pith removed, seeded, segmented and cut in half
1 × 425 g can sliced peaches, drained	1 × 15 oz can sliced peaches, drained
a few grapes	a few grapes
½ cucumber, chopped	½ cucumber, chopped
1 × 425 g can pineapple chunks, drained	1 × 15 oz can pineapple chunks, drained
1 × 425 g can guavas, drained and lightly mashed	1 × 15 oz can guavas, drained and lightly mashed
about 1 × 2.5 ml spoon chilli powder	about ½ teaspoon chilli powder
1–2 × 5 ml spoons freshly ground black pepper	1–2 teaspoons freshly ground black pepper
pinch of salt or black salt	pinch of salt or black salt
1 small ripe pawpaw, peeled, seeds removed and cubed, or 1 × 425 g can pawpaw, drained and cubed	1 small ripe pawpaw, peeled, seeds removed and cubed, or 1 × 15 oz can pawpaw, drained and cubed
lemon juice, to taste	lemon juice, to taste

Preparation time: 15 minutes

In a large bowl mix together the apple, banana, pear, orange, peaches, grapes, cucumber, pineapple and guavas. Sprinkle with the chilli powder, pepper and salt. Add the cubed pawpaw and sprinkle with lemon juice. Toss all the fruits well.
Serve this savoury fruit salad with Kebabs (page 33) or Samosas (page 15).

Hari chutney (green chutney)

Metric
50 g tamarind pods or 100 g green unripe mango flesh
175 g fresh or desiccated coconut
4–6 large or 8–10 small sprigs of coriander leaves, stalks discarded
1–2 green chillis, seeded and roughly chopped
25 g fresh ginger root, peeled
1 × 5 ml spoon cumin seeds
1 × 2.5–5 ml spoon salt
1 small onion, peeled and finely chopped

Imperial
2 oz tamarind pods or 4 oz green unripe mango flesh
6 oz fresh or desiccated coconut
4–6 large or 8–10 small sprigs of coriander leaves, stalks discarded
1–2 green chillis, seeded and roughly chopped
1 oz fresh ginger root, peeled
1 teaspoon cumin seeds
½–1 teaspoon salt
1 small onion, peeled and finely chopped

Preparation time: 30–50 minutes

Green chutney is popular in all parts of India. Sometimes local produce is added. Apart from being a good accompaniment to Indian food it can be spread on pieces of bread and made into a delicious sandwich.

Soak the tamarind pods in two teacups of hot water for 10–15 minutes and extract the pulp. Repeat this process to extract any remaining pulp.
Grind the coconut, coriander leaves, chilli, ginger, cumin seeds and tamarind pulp to a smooth paste. If using the mango add a little water. Add salt and stir in the chopped onion.
Serve with a main dish or with savoury snacks.

From the left: Hari chutney; Hara dhania chutney; Til copra chutney

Til copra chutney (sesame seed and onion chutney)

Metric
100 g tamarind pods
100 g sesame seeds,
    dry roasted
100 g fresh or desiccated
    coconut
1 green chilli, seeded
    and roughly chopped
3–4 sprigs of coriander
    leaves, stalks
    discarded
1 × 5 ml spoon salt
1 medium onion, peeled
    and thinly sliced
a little water or lemon
    juice (optional)

Imperial
4 oz tamarind pods
4 oz sesame seeds,
    dry roasted
4 oz fresh or desiccated
    coconut
1 green chilli, seeded
    and roughly chopped
3–4 sprigs of coriander
    leaves, stalks
    discarded
1 teaspoon salt
1 medium onion, peeled
    and thinly sliced
a little water or lemon
    juice (optional)

Preparation time: 10–15 minutes

Soak the tamarind pods in four teacups of hot water for 10–15 minutes and extract the pulp. Repeat this process to extract any remaining pulp. Grind the sesame seeds, coconut, chilli, coriander and tamarind pulp to a smooth paste. Add the salt and stir in the sliced onion.
If the chutney is too thick add a little water or lemon juice or a mixture of both.
Serve with a main dish, with savoury snacks or spread on slices of bread to make sandwiches.

Variation:
Grind two garlic cloves, peeled, in with the other ingredients.

Hara dhania chutney (coriander chutney)

Metric
50 g tamarind pods or
    150 ml plain
    unsweetened yogurt
1 small onion, peeled and
    sliced (optional)
8–10 large or 12–15 small
    sprigs of coriander
    leaves, stalks discarded
25 g fresh ginger root,
    peeled and chopped
2 × 5 ml spoons cumin seeds
5–6 sprigs fresh mint leaves
    or 1 × 15 ml spoon dried
    mint
1½–2 × 15 ml spoons sugar
1–2 green chillis, seeded
    and roughly chopped
1 × 2.5 ml spoon salt

Imperial
2 oz tamarind pods or ¼
    pint plain unsweetened
    yogurt
1 small onion, peeled and
    sliced (optional)
8–10 large or 12–15 small
    sprigs of coriander
    leaves, stalks discarded
1 oz fresh ginger root,
    peeled and chopped
2 teaspoons cumin seeds
5–6 sprigs fresh mint leaves
    or 1 tablespoon dried
    mint
1½–2 tablespoons sugar
1–2 green chillis, seeded
    and roughly chopped
½ teaspoon salt

Preparation time: about 35 minutes

If using tamarind soak the pods in two teacups of hot water for 10–15 minutes and extract the pulp. Repeat this process to extract any remaining pulp. Place all the ingredients in a blender goblet and blend until smooth. Taste and add more sugar or salt if necessary.

Variation:
To make a sour chutney use only 2 × 5 ml/2 teaspoons sugar and include 2 × 5 ml/2 teaspoons salt.

Tarkari ki chutney (mixed vegetable chutney)

Preparation time: 35–45 minutes
Cooking time: about 35 minutes

This chutney should be eaten within seven days.

Metric
25 g tamarind pods
2 × 15 ml spoons oil
1 × 5 ml spoon mustard
　seeds
1 small onion, peeled
　and diced
1 medium sweet potato,
　peeled and diced
　(optional)
1 carrot, peeled and
　diced
50 g sweetcorn
1 kg tomatoes,
　skinned and chopped
1 × 5 ml spoon salt
about 1 × 5 ml spoon chilli
　powder
1 × 2.5 ml spoon ground
　turmeric
50 g fresh ginger root,
　peeled and grated
3 × 15 ml spoons soft
　brown sugar
200 ml malt vinegar
100 g sultanas and
　raisins
75 ml water
1/2 cucumber, chopped
　and juice discarded

Imperial
1 oz tamarind pods
2 tablespoons oil
1 teaspoon mustard
　seeds
1 small onion, peeled
　and diced
1 medium sweet potato,
　peeled and diced
　(optional)
1 carrot, peeled and
　diced
2 oz sweetcorn
2 lb tomatoes,
　skinned and chopped
1 teaspoon salt
about 1 teaspoon chilli
　powder
1/2 teaspoon ground
　turmeric
2 oz fresh ginger root,
　peeled and grated
3 tablespoons soft
　brown sugar
1/3 pint malt vinegar
4 oz sultanas and
　raisins
3 fl oz water
1/2 cucumber, chopped
　and juice discarded

Soak the tamarind pods in a teacup of hot water for 10–15 minutes and extract the pulp. Repeat this process to extract any remaining pulp.
Heat the oil in a pan and fry the mustard seeds. When they begin to crackle add the onion, sweet potato, carrot and sweetcorn, and fry for 4–5 minutes. Add the tomatoes, salt and chilli powder, cover and simmer until the tomatoes are soft.
Stir in the turmeric, grated ginger, sugar, vinegar, tamarind pulp, raisins and sultanas. Gently simmer until the sugar syrup is thick and the vegetables are tender, adding a little water if necessary. Add the cucumber and simmer for 1 minute. Allow to cool.

Khubani ki chutney; Tarkari ki chutney

Khubani ki chutney (apricot chutney)

Metric
225 g dried apricots,
   soaked overnight
150 ml vinegar
250 g sugar
25 g fresh ginger root,
   peeled and crushed
4 garlic cloves, peeled
   and crushed
   (optional)
about 1 × 5 ml spoon chilli
   powder
pinch of salt

Imperial
8 oz dried apricots,
   soaked overnight
¼ pint vinegar
9 oz sugar
1 oz fresh ginger root,
   peeled and crushed
4 garlic cloves, peeled
   and crushed
   (optional)
about 1 teaspoon chilli
   powder
pinch of salt

Preparation time: 10 minutes, plus overnight soaking
Cooking time: about 55 minutes

Place the apricots and the soaking liquid with enough water to cover in a saucepan. Simmer until tender then beat or blend to a smooth consistency.

In a separate pan place the vinegar, sugar, crushed ginger and garlic, chilli powder and salt. Heat gently, stirring, until the sugar has dissolved, then increase the heat until a syrup is formed.

Stir the apricots into the syrup and simmer gently for about 10 minutes to the desired thickness. Allow to cool and bottle in airtight jars with vinegar-proof tops.

RICE AND BREAD

The best variety of rice to use in savoury dishes is basmati. It has a distinct aroma and flavour hence its name which means 'the fragrant one'. The next choice should be long-grain American and the other popular variety used is patna rice, which is grown in the Bengal and Bihar district of India. The long fat grains of the latter are more starchy than the former varieties.

Whichever type of rice you choose to cook with, remember that it increases 2–3 times in volume when cooked. Before cooking the rice rinse it in several changes of warm water until the water is clear, rubbing the rice very gently between your palms and removing any pieces of husk. This stage is not necessary if using long-grain American rice.

There are many different types of Indian bread, all of which are interchangeable and can be chosen according to taste. When kneaded with fat and made into thin pancake-like wafers they are called chappatis. Flat (unleavened) bread is called roti. There are shallow-fried parathas, deep-fried puris, and baked nan.

Nan; Tahiri

Nan or khamiri roti (leavened bread)

Metric	Imperial
1 × 2.5 ml spoon dried yeast	½ teaspoon dried yeast
1 × 5 ml spoon sugar	1 teaspoon sugar
120 ml lukewarm milk or water	4 fl oz lukewarm milk or water
450 g plain white flour	1 lb plain white flour
1 × 2.5 ml spoon salt	½ teaspoon salt
1 × 5 ml baking powder	1 teaspoon baking powder
1 × 15 ml spoon plain unsweetened yogurt	1 tablespoon plain unsweetened yogurt
25 g butter or ghee	1 oz butter or ghee
melted butter or ghee	melted butter or ghee
sesame seeds (optional)	sesame seeds (optional)

Preparation time: 45 minutes, plus 4–5 hours for rising
Cooking time: 6–8 minutes
Oven: 190°C, 375°F, Gas Mark 5

Stir the yeast and sugar into the milk or water and leave covered for 10–15 minutes in a warm place until the liquid is frothy.
Sift the flour, salt and baking powder together and make a well in the centre. Add the yogurt and 25 g/ 1 oz butter or ghee and mix to a soft dough, gradually adding the yeast solution, and a little extra milk or water if necessary. Cover and set aside for 4–5 hours. Knead well for 1–2 minutes. Divide the dough into 18–20 balls and roll out on a floured surface. Brush the shapes with the melted butter or ghee and sprinkle with sesame seeds. Place on baking trays and cook in a preheated oven for 3–4 minutes on both sides until brown specks appear.
Makes 18–20

Tahiri (vegetable pulao)

Metric	Imperial
50 g ghee or butter	2 oz ghee or butter
1 small onion, peeled and chopped	1 small onion, peeled and chopped

Garam masala:	Garam masala:
4–6 small green cardamoms	4–6 small green cardamoms
2–3 large cardamoms	2–3 large cardamoms
6 cloves	6 cloves
1 bay leaf	1 bay leaf
1 × 1 cm stick cinnamon	1 × ½ inch stick cinnamon
1 × 5 ml spoon black cumin seeds	1 teaspoon black cumin seeds
50 g peas	2 oz peas
2 teacups basmati rice, rinsed and drained	2 teacups basmati rice, rinsed and drained
about 1½ × 5 ml spoons salt	about 1½ teaspoons salt
4 teacups water	4 teacups water

Preparation time: 20 minutes
Cooking time: 30 minutes

A pulao differs from a biryani by not containing hot spices. Although there are various types of pulao the flavouring is usually done with onions and a garam masala. All pulaos can be coloured by a weak solution of food colouring or by adding ground turmeric or saffron, used sparingly.

Melt the ghee or butter in a large pan and fry the onion until golden brown. Lower the heat and add the cardamoms, cloves, bay leaf, cinnamon and cumin seeds. Fry for 30 seconds and add the peas. Fry for 1 minute, then add the rice. Sprinkle with salt and stir gently a few times.
Add the water, bring to the boil and stir briefly. Cover and cook on a very low heat without stirring for 10–15 minutes until the water is fully absorbed.
If the rice is not fully cooked by the time the water is fully absorbed add about 1 × 15 ml spoon/1 tablespoon warm water and continue cooking.
Transfer to a serving dish and lightly separate the grains of rice with a fork.

Variations:
Instead of peas use 50 g/2 oz mixed unsalted nuts and sultanas, raisins or dates. Cashew nuts, almonds or pistachio nuts are usually used. Do not use walnuts, pecan nuts, or hazelnuts because they contain strong, aromatic oils.
Add roughly chopped cauliflower and potato and fry for 3–4 minutes before adding the garam masala.

Biryani 1 (meat and rice)

Metric
75 g ghee or butter
1 onion, peeled and sliced
1 bay leaf
1 × 1 cm stick cinnamon
4 small green cardamoms
2 large cardamoms
6 cloves
450 g meat, cubed
2 × 5 ml spoons ginger
    paste or ground ginger
2 × 5 ml spoons garlic
    paste or garlic powder
1 × 2.5 ml spoon ground
    turmeric
2 × 5 ml spoons ground
    coriander
2 × 5 ml spoons ground
    cumin
150 ml plain unsweetened
    yogurt
1 × 5 ml spoon salt
about 1 × 5 ml spoon
    chilli powder
450 ml water

To cook the rice:
750 g rice
2.25–2.75 litres water
2 × 5 ml spoons salt
1 bay leaf
1 × 1 cm stick cinnamon
1 × 5 ml spoon black
    cumin seeds

To finish:
1 small onion, peeled,
    sliced and fried
3–4 sprigs of coriander
    leaves, chopped
2 green chillis, seeded
    and very finely
    chopped
freshly ground black pepper
4 small green cardamoms,
    ground
juice of 2 lemons
yellow food colouring
    or a pinch of ground
    saffron dissolved in
    water
3 × 15 ml spoons milk
25 g butter or ghee,
    melted

Imperial
3 oz ghee or butter
1 onion, peeled and sliced
1 bay leaf
1 × ½ inch stick cinnamon
4 small green cardamoms
2 large cardamoms
6 cloves
1 lb meat, cubed
2 teaspoons ginger
    paste or ground ginger
2 teaspoons garlic
    paste or garlic powder
½ teaspoon ground
    turmeric
2 teaspoons ground
    coriander
2 teaspoons ground
    cumin
¼ pint plain unsweetened
    yogurt
1 teaspoon salt
about 1 teaspoon
    chilli powder
¾ pint water

To cook the rice:
1½ lb rice
4–5 pints water
2 teaspoons salt
1 bay leaf
1 × ½ inch stick cinnamon
1 teaspoon black cumin
    seeds

To finish:
1 small onion, peeled,
    sliced and fried
3–4 sprigs of coriander
    leaves, chopped
2 green chillis, seeded
    and very finely
    chopped
freshly ground black pepper
4 small green cardamoms,
    ground
juice of 2 lemons
yellow food colouring
    or a pinch of ground
    saffron dissolved in
    water
3 tablespoons milk
1 oz butter or ghee,
    melted

Preparation time: 40 minutes
Cooking time: 2 hours

There are two methods of cooking biryani. Both are easy and very effective in producing the unique result. In this method, the meat and rice are cooked separately, then layered. This ensures that the rice will be cooked to perfection. Any type of rice can be used but basmati is the best. A simple raita, salad or chutney is often enough accompaniment and in restaurants a curry sauce is often presented as a side dish.

Melt the ghee or butter in a large pan and fry the onion until golden. Add the bay leaf, cinnamon, cardamoms and cloves. Fry for 1 minute. Add the meat, ginger, garlic, turmeric, coriander, cumin, yogurt, salt and chilli powder, and stir well. Cover and cook until dry. Increase the heat and fry until the oil separates from the mixture. Add the water and continue cooking for 40–50 minutes until the meat is tender. There should be about 3 × 15 ml spoons/3 tablespoons thick sauce. Meanwhile cook the rice. Place it in a large saucepan, add the water, salt, bay leaf, cinnamon stick and black cumin seeds. Bring to the boil and cook the rice until it is almost tender. Remove from the heat and drain.
Put a thin layer of rice in the base of a clean, heavy-based pan. Spread over a layer of cooked meat, without the sauce, followed by layers of fried onion, chopped coriander leaves and chilli. Repeat the layers once or twice, retaining a little onion and chopped coriander and finishing with a layer of rice.
Sprinkle the surface with fried onion, chopped coriander, pepper, cardamom and the lemon juice. With a spoon handle make three or four holes in the rice to allow the steam to rise and pour the food colouring or saffron, remaining sauce, milk and butter or ghee at random over the surface. Place the pan on a medium heat and as soon as any steam is visible, lower the heat, cover and cook very gently for 5 minutes.
To serve, use a wide spoon and from one edge scoop out and mix a portion of the rice and meat together.

Biryani 2 (meat and rice)

Preparation time: 30 minutes
Cooking time: about 1 hour
Oven: 160°C, 325°F, Gas Mark 3

In this method, known as kachhi handi ki biryani, the rice is partially cooked and then added to and cooked with the marinated meat.

Melt the ghee or butter in a pan and fry the onion until golden brown. Add the cinnamon stick, bay leaf, cardamoms, cloves and fry for 1 minute. Remove from the heat. Stir in the garlic, ginger, chilli powder, cumin, coriander, turmeric, meat, yogurt and salt, cover and set aside.

Meanwhile pour the water into a large saucepan and add the rice, black cumin seeds, cinnamon, bay leaf and salt. Bring to the boil and cook for 5–7 minutes until the rice is half cooked. It should still feel firm but have soaked up some water. Drain well.

Transfer the meat mixture to a large casserole dish and level the surface. Spread the rice evenly on top. Sprinkle with the fried onions, chopped coriander, green chilli, lemon juice and milk. Make three or four holes with a spoon handle to allow the steam to rise, and pour the food colouring or saffon at random over the surface. Cover and cook in a preheated oven for 50–60 minutes. When both the rice and meat are cooked, mix them together before serving.

Variation:
Add a few drops of rose or kewra water for flavouring, mixed in with the food colouring.

Metric
100 g ghee or butter
1 onion, peeled and sliced
1 × 1 cm stick cinnamon
1 bay leaf
4 small green cardamoms
2 large cardamoms
6 cloves
2 × 5 ml spoons garlic paste
    or garlic powder
2 × 5 ml spoons ginger
    paste or ground ginger
about 1 × 5 ml spoon chilli
    powder
2 × 5 ml spoons ground
    cumin
2 × 5 ml spoons ground
    coriander
1 × 2.5 ml spoon ground
    turmeric
450 g meat, cubed
150 ml plain unsweetened
    yogurt
1 × 5 ml spoon salt

To cook the rice:
2.25–2.75 litres water
750 g rice
1 × 5 ml spoon black cumin
    seeds
1 × 1 cm stick cinnamon
1 bay leaf

To finish:
1 small onion, peeled,
    sliced and fried
chopped coriander leaves
2 green chillis, halved and
    seeded
juice of 2 lemons
25 ml milk
food colouring or ground
    saffron dissolved
    in water

Imperial
4 oz ghee or butter
1 onion, peeled and sliced
1 × ½ inch stick cinnamon
1 bay leaf
4 small green cardamoms
2 large cardamoms
6 cloves
2 teaspoons garlic
    paste or garlic powder
2 teaspoons ginger
    paste or ground ginger
about 1 teaspoon chilli
    powder
2 teaspoons ground
    cumin
2 teaspoons ground
    coriander
½ teaspoon ground
    turmeric
1 lb meat, cubed
¼ pint plain
    unsweetened yogurt
1 teaspoon salt

To cook the rice:
4–5 pints water
1½ lb rice
1 teaspoon black cumin
    seeds
1 × ½ inch stick cinnamon
1 bay leaf

To finish:
1 small onion, peeled,
    sliced and fried
chopped coriander leaves
2 green chillis, halved
    and seeded
juice of 2 lemons
1 fl oz milk
food colouring or ground
    saffron dissolved
    in water

Left: Biryani 1; Right: Biryani 2

Sada pulao (plain fried rice)

Metric
75 g ghee or butter
1 small onion, peeled
  and chopped
2 teacups long-grain
  American or basmati
  rice, rinsed and drained
1 × 5 ml spoon salt
4 teacups water

Imperial
3 oz ghee or butter
1 small onion, peeled
  and chopped
2 teacups long-grain
  American or basmati
  rice, rinsed and drained
1 teaspoon salt
4 teacups water

Preparation time: 15 minutes
Cooking time: 30 minutes

Plain fried rice is eaten in one form or another all over the Asian Continent. The rice is usually cooked in oil tempered with whole garam masala, and cumin seeds or onion. When cooked with fish, meat and poultry it is called pulao or biryani, with pulses it is called khichhari (kedgeree), and with vegetables it is called tahiri, pulao, or pilaf.

Melt the ghee or butter in a large pan. Fry the chopped onion until golden brown. Add the rice and salt, and fry for ½–1 minute.
Add the water, cover and bring to the boil. Lower the heat and gently stir the rice a few times. Cover and cook on a very gentle heat for 10–15 minutes until the water is fully absorbed and the rice is cooked. Do not stir during the cooking. If the rice is not cooked by the time the water is fully absorbed, add 1 × 15 ml spoon/ 1 tablespoon warm water and continue cooking until the rice is tender.

Variations:
Add 1 × 5 ml/1 teaspoon black cumin seeds or the following whole garam masala, with or without the onion, and fry for 1 minute before adding the rice: add 4 small green cardamoms, 2 large cardamoms, 1 × 5 ml spoon/1 teaspoon black cumin seeds, 4 cloves, 8–10 peppercorns, 1 × 1 cm/½ inch stick cinnamon, and 1 bay leaf.
To make egg fried rice, pour two beaten eggs over the nearly-cooked rice. Do not stir until the rice is fully cooked and the water is absorbed.

Pulao gosht (meat pulao)

Metric
50 g ghee or butter
1 small onion, peeled and
  chopped
1 bay leaf
1 × 1 cm stick cinnamon
4 small green cardamoms
2 large cardamoms
1 × 5 ml spoon black cumin
  seeds
4 cloves
8 black peppercorns
450 g meat, cubed
about 1 × 5 ml spoon
  salt
1.6 litres water
450 g basmati rice,
  rinsed and drained

Imperial
2 oz ghee or butter
1 small onion, peeled
  and chopped
1 bay leaf
1 × ½ inch stick cinnamon
4 small green cardamoms
2 large cardamoms
1 teaspoon black cumin
  seeds
4 cloves
8 black peppercorns
1 lb meat, cubed
about 1 teaspoon
  salt
2¾ pints water
1 lb basmati rice,
  rinsed and drained

Preparation time: 15 minutes
Cooking time: about 1 hour 10 minutes

In a meat pulao the meat is cooked with the spices, then the rice is added. To enhance the appearance and flavour, nuts, peas or pineapple can be added and a pulao may be coloured with a weak orange food colouring solution or saffron.

Melt the ghee or butter in a large pan and fry the onion until golden brown. Add all the spices and fry for 1 minute. Add the meat and salt and fry for 2–3 minutes. Stir in the water. Cover and simmer gently for 40–50 minutes until the meat is tender, and the liquid has reduced to about two-thirds its original amount. If the quantity is less than this add a little extra water.
Stir the rice in with the meat and cook on a gentle heat without stirring until the rice is tender and the mixture is dry.

Variations:
100 g/4 oz of mixed unsalted nuts and raisins, or peas, or potatoes can be added during the cooking, keeping in mind the time it takes for these ingredients to cook. To make chicken or prawn pulao substitute chicken pieces or 225 g/8 oz peeled prawns for the meat. The prawns will only need to be added for the last 10–15 minutes of the cooking time.

From the left, clockwise: Sada pulao;
Ubley chawal; Pulao gosht

Ubley chawal 1 (plain boiled rice)

Metric
2.25–2.75 litres cold
   water
1 × 2.5 ml spoon salt
few drops of lemon
   juice (optional)
350 g rice, rinsed and
   drained

Imperial
4–5 pints cold
   water
½ teaspoon salt
few drops of lemon
   juice (optional)
12 oz rice, rinsed and
   drained

Preparation time: 5 minutes
Cooking time: 15 minutes

This method of cooking rice in a large quantity of water is suitable for every type and produces fluffy and starch-free rice. Lemon juice can be included and this will whiten the rice.

Fill a large saucepan with the cold water. Add the salt, lemon juice and rice. Bring to the boil and simmer until the grains are almost cooked. The rice should still have a firm centre.
Drain, cover and place the saucepan on a very low heat for 2 minutes. The moisture left around the rice will be enough to cook the centre.
Serve plain or with melted ghee or butter. For a simple light meal serve with a daal.
Serves 4

Ubley chawal 2 (plain boiled rice)

Metric
4 teacups water
1 × 2.5 ml spoon salt
few drops of lemon
   juice (optional)
2 teacups long-grain
   American or basmati
   rice, rinsed and drained

Imperial
4 teacups water
½ teaspoon salt
few drops of lemon
   juice (optional)
2 teacups long-grain
   American or basmati
   rice, rinsed and drained

Preparation time: 5 minutes
Cooking time: 15 minutes

This second method is only suitable for high quality rice, such as basmati rice or long-grain American rice. As the starch content is lower in these types they can be cooked with a measured amount of water, which is completely absorbed during cooking. If preferred, soak the rice in the water for 10–15 minutes and cook it for half the time.

Bring the water to the boil in a large saucepan. Add the salt, lemon juice and the rice. Bring to the boil, stir briefly, cover and simmer for 8–12 minutes until the water is absorbed. Do not stir during cooking. Keep on a very low heat for a further 1–2 minutes.
Serve plain or with melted butter or ghee.
Serves 4

Kachori (stuffed deep-fried bread)

Metric
450 g plain wholemeal flour
1 × 2.5 ml spoon salt
120–175 ml water

Imperial
1 lb plain wholemeal flour
½ teaspoon salt
4–6 fl oz water

Urid daal filling:
100 g urid daal, washed
  and soaked for 3 hours
1 × 5 ml spoon cumin
  seeds
1 × 5 ml spoon aniseed
2 × 15 ml spoons oil
pinch of asafoetida
  (optional)
1 green chilli, seeded
  and very finely
  chopped, or 1 × 5 ml
  spoon chilli powder
pinch of salt
oil for deep frying

Urid daal filling:
4 oz urid daal, washed
  and soaked for 3 hours
1 teaspoon cumin
  seeds
1 teaspoon aniseed
2 tablespoons oil
pinch of asafoetida
  (optional)
1 green chilli, seeded
  and very finely
  chopped, or 1 teaspoon
  chilli powder
pinch of salt
oil for deep frying

Preparation time: 30 minutes, plus 3 hours soaking
Cooking time: 40–50 minutes

Mix the flour and salt together and make a well in the centre. Gradually add the water to make a dough. Knead well for 1–2 minutes, cover and set aside.
To make the urid daal filling, drain and grind the urid daal to a thick coarse paste with a little water. Dry roast the cumin seeds and aniseed for ½ minute and grind coarsely. Heat the oil in a pan and sprinkle in the asafoetida and urid daal mixture. Sprinkle with the chilli, salt, and ground cumin and aniseed. Fry for 5 minutes, adding a little extra oil if necessary. Allow to go cold.
Divide the dough into 25–28 portions. Roll one portion into a ball and make a depression in the middle. Press about 1 × 5 ml spoon/1 teaspoon filling in the depression and shape the dough into a ball to enclose the filling. Carefully roll out into a 7.5 cm/ 3 inch circle. Make the remaining kachoris similarly. Heat 5–6 cm/2–2½ inches of oil in a deep frying pan and fry the kachoris a few at a time until golden brown on both sides. Keep warm.
Serve hot with a chutney or tomato ketchup.
Makes 25–28

Variations:
To make potato kachoris, peel, boil and mash 100 g/ 4 oz potatoes and add salt and pepper or chilli powder. Knead into the dough, divide into portions, roll out and fry. To make green pea kachoris, lightly mash 100 g/4 oz uncooked peas and 15 g/½ oz fresh ginger root, peeled and chopped. Substitute for the daal.

Puri (deep-fried bread)

Metric
450 g plain wholemeal flour
1 × 2.5 ml spoon salt
about 120–175 ml water
oil for deep frying

Imperial
1 lb plain wholemeal flour
½ teaspoon salt
about 4–6 fl oz water
oil for deep frying

Preparation time: 20 minutes
Cooking time: about 30 minutes

When frying puris there are two important points. First, the oil should be the right temperature and secondly, the second side needs longer frying so that the puri swells up.

Mix the flour and salt together and make a well in the centre. Gradually add the water to make a dough. Knead well for 1–2 minutes and set aside, covered, for 5 minutes.
Divide the dough into 25–28 portions. Roll each portion into a flat 7.5 cm/3 inch round.
Heat 5–6 cm/2–2½ inches of oil in a deep frying pan and drop a small amount of flour into the oil. If it floats to the surface and turns light brown the oil is at the correct temperature. Slide in one puri at a time and fry on both sides until light brown. It will quickly swell up in the oil.
Lift out the puri with a slotted spoon and drain on kitchen paper. Continue frying the puris and stack one on top of the other, alternating the thin and thick sides so as to prevent sticking. Keep wrapped in a tea towel or place in a covered container.
To keep puris warm for a longer period, wrap them in aluminium foil and put inside a covered container. If puris are left uncovered they become crisp, and unsuitable for eating with curries.
Makes 25–28

Variations:
Add either 1 × 5 ml spoon/1 teaspoon onion seeds, or 1 × 2.5 ml spoon/½ teaspoon chilli powder to the dough or to make green puris, add 2 × 15 ml spoons/2 tablespoons spinach purée.
About 25 g/1 oz ghee may be mixed into the dough to make softer puris.
Use a mixture of wholemeal and plain white flour.

From the left: Puris; Green pea kachoris; Kachoris

Paratha
(shallow-fried bread)

Metric
450 g plain wholemeal flour
pinch of salt
about 120–175 ml water
melted ghee or butter

Imperial
1 lb plain wholemeal flour
pinch of salt
about 4–6 fl oz water
melted ghee or butter

Preparation time: 15 minutes
Cooking time: about 30 minutes

Parathas are brushed with melted ghee or butter and then shallow fried. Sometimes they contain a meat or vegetable filling and they can be triangular, square or round. The dough will keep in a refrigerator for up to one week.

Mix the flour and salt together and make a well in the centre. Gradually add enough water to make a soft dough and knead well until no longer sticky. Divide into 16 portions.
On a floured surface, roll each portion into a flat round and brush ghee or butter all over the surface. Fold in half and brush with ghee or butter and fold again into a small triangle. Roll out thinly with a little extra flour. Alternatively to make round parathas roll each portion into a 13–15 cm/5–6 inch round and brush with ghee or butter. Then fold in a little at one edge and roll each portion into a tube shape. Hold the shape upright and flatten it into a ball. Roll out thinly with a little extra wholemeal flour.
Gently heat a frying pan or Indian bread pan and place a portion in it. Cook on each side for 1–2 minutes. Brush 1 × 5 ml spoon/1 teaspoon melted ghee or butter over the surface, turn the shape over and gently fry until golden brown. Repeat with the second side. Remove from the pan and keep wrapped in a tea towel, or place in a covered container. Cook the remaining parathas and stack one on top of the other.
Makes 16

Variations:
To make stuffed parathas, roll one portion into a ball and make a depression in the middle. Press about 1 × 5 ml spoon/1 teaspoon of a dry mince curry (see Keema page 35), or a dry vegetable curry, into the depression and shape the dough into a ball to enclose the filling. Carefully roll out into a 7.5 cm/3 inch circle. Fill the remaining portions similarly and fry them as above.
Grated raw cauliflower, onion or radish can be used as fillings, seasoned with salt, chilli powder and ground cumin seeds, to taste.

Roti or chappati
(wholemeal bread)

Metric
450 g plain wholemeal flour
pinch of salt
about 120–175 ml water
melted ghee or butter

Imperial
1 lb plain wholemeal flour
pinch of salt
about 4–6 fl oz water
melted ghee or butter

Preparation time: 15 minutes
Cooking time: about 30 minutes

This bread does not contain any fat in the dough, instead it is brushed with melted ghee or butter after it has been cooked. The dough for these will keep in a refrigerator for up to one week.

Sift the flour and salt together. Make a well in the centre and gradually add enough water to make a soft dough. Knead well until no longer sticky.
Shape the dough into 24 small balls. On a floured surface, roll out each ball into an 18 cm/7 inch round. Gently heat a frying pan or Indian bread pan and place a round of dough in it. When little brown specks appear on the underside, turn the round over and cook briefly on the other side. Flip the roti over again and with a clean tea towel, press gently to circulate steam all around, until the underside is golden brown. Cook the other side similarly. Remove and place on a plate. Brush melted ghee or butter over the top of the roti and keep wrapped in a tea towel, or place in a covered container. Cook the remaining rotis and stack one on top of the other.
Makes 24

Variations:
A mixture of plain white flour and wholemeal flour may be used.
After cooking them on both sides the rotis can be placed under a preheated grill. When the roti swells, turn it over and cook the other side for about ½ minute.

Rogani roti (rich bread)

Metric	*Imperial*
450 g plain wholemeal flour	*1 lb plain wholemeal flour*
pinch of salt	*pinch of salt*
150 ml milk	*¼ pint milk*
50 g butter or 50 ml cream	*2 oz butter or 2 fl oz cream*
ghee or butter for	*ghee or butter for*
frying (optional)	*frying (optional)*

Preparation time: 15 minutes
Cooking time: about 30 minutes

'Rogan' means creamy and rogani roti is made with milk and butter or cream. This type of bread is usually soft and keeps well for a few days. In India it is often given to elderly people who may find it difficult to eat the firmer breads. Rogani roti also makes good use of any leftover cream.

Mix the flour and salt together and make a well in the centre. Warm the milk slightly and melt the butter in it, but do not allow the milk to boil. Gradually add the milk and butter, or milk and cream, to the flour. Knead well for 1–2 minutes.
Divide the dough into 22–24 portions. On a floured surface roll one portion into a 13–15 cm/5–6 inch circle about 5 mm/¼ inch thick.
Gently heat a frying pan or Indian bread pan and place the circle in it. Over a medium heat cook the dough on both sides until brown specks appear. Then either press the roti with a clean tea towel or add 1 × 5 ml spoon/1 teaspoon ghee or butter and cook briefly until golden brown on both sides. Remove from the pan and keep wrapped in a tea towel, or place in a covered container. Cook the remaining rotis and stack one on top of the other.
Makes 22–24

Variations:
A combination of yogurt and cream, or all soured cream, or evaporated milk may be used instead of the milk mixture.
A mixture of plain white flour and wholemeal flour may be used.

From the front: Rotis; Rogani rotis; Parathas

SWEETS

Most Indians end their meal with a sweet which is invariably milk-based. Due to the excessive heat in many parts of India and general lack of refrigerating facilities, fresh milk cannot be easily stored. This is why the sweets are usually made from a form of condensed milk, which can be kept for long periods without refrigeration and this ensures an adequate supply of dairy produce in the diet. Powdered milk is a good alternative in this country.

Indian sweets are very rich, but a small portion is a delicious way to finish a meal. If possible use a non-stick saucepan when preparing these sweets, as some of them stick to the pan easily.

Gajjar ka halwa; Gulab jaman; Rawa halwa

Gajjar ka halwa (carrot pudding)

Metric	Imperial
450 g carrots, peeled and grated	1 lb carrots, peeled and grated
175–225 g sugar	6–8 oz sugar
900 ml milk	1½ pints milk
50 g butter or ghee	2 oz butter or ghee
25 g sultanas or raisins	1 oz sultanas or raisins
8 small green cardamoms, shelled and seeds ground	8 small green cardamoms, shelled and seeds ground
15 g almonds, blanched and sliced	½ oz almonds, blanched and sliced
15 g pistachio nuts, sliced or chopped	½ oz pistachio nuts, sliced or chopped

Preparation time: 30 minutes
Cooking time: 1½–2 hours

Put the grated carrots, sugar and milk in a nonstick or heavy-based pan. Cover and cook gently for 1–1½ hours until the liquid has evaporated.

Add the butter or ghee and sultanas or raisins, increase the heat and fry for about 20 minutes, stirring constantly to prevent the mixture sticking to the base of the pan. During this stage the colour will darken. Remove from the heat and add the ground cardamom seeds. Mix well and pour into a serving dish. Smooth the surface with a wet spatula and sprinkle the nuts evenly on top. Serve hot or cold.

Gulab jaman (milk balls in syrup)

Metric	*Imperial*
350 g sugar	12 oz sugar
750 ml water	1¼ pints water
4 drops rose or kewra water	4 drops rose or kewra water
7 × 15 ml spoons low fat powdered milk	7 tablespoons low fat powdered milk
3 × 5 ml spoons self-raising flour	3 teaspoons self-raising flour
1 × 5 ml spoon semolina	1 teaspoon semolina
3 × 5 ml spoons ghee	3 teaspoons ghee
8 small green cardamoms, shelled and seeds ground	8 small green cardamoms, shelled and seeds ground
pinch of saffron	pinch of saffron
milk to mix	milk to mix
oil for deep frying	oil for deep frying

Preparation time: 20 minutes
Cooking time: 20 minutes

Put the sugar and water in a heavy-based or nonstick pan and heat gently to dissolve the sugar. Increase the heat and boil for 2–3 minutes to make a syrup. Stir in the rose or kewra water and set aside.
Put the powdered milk, flour, semolina, ghee, ground cardamom seeds, and saffron into a bowl. Mix well with a little milk to make a soft dough. Divide into 20–22 equal portions, and roll each portion into a ball. Heat the oil and gently deep fry the balls over a low heat until golden brown. Remove with a slotted spoon and transfer to the syrup. When all the balls are fried bring the syrup to boiling point, then remove from the heat. Serve hot or cold.

Rawa halwa (semolina pudding)

Metric	*Imperial*
175 g coarse semolina	6 oz coarse semolina
175 g unsalted butter or ghee	6 oz unsalted butter or ghee
100 g sugar	4 oz sugar
10–15 small green cardamoms, shelled and seeds ground	10–15 small green cardamoms, shelled and seeds ground
25 g blanched almonds, sliced	1 oz blanched almonds, sliced
25 g sultanas or raisins	1 oz sultanas or raisins
450 ml water or milk	¾ pint water or milk
almonds and sultanas, to garnish	almonds and sultanas, to garnish

Preparation time: 10 minutes
Cooking time: 20 minutes

In a heavy-based or nonstick pan gently dry roast the semolina until light brown. Add the butter or ghee and fry for 5–7 minutes, stirring, until golden brown. Over a low heat, stir in the sugar, ground cardamom seeds, almonds, and sultanas or raisins. Gently fry for 1 minute, stirring constantly. Stir in the water or milk, cover and leave on a low heat for 1–2 minutes. Stir, then increase the heat and cook for 2–3 minutes until the mixture is thick. Serve hot or cold.

Chawal ki kheer (rice pudding)

Metric	Imperial
1 × 5 ml spoon ghee or butter	1 teaspoon ghee or butter
1 × 1 cm stick cinnamon	1 × ½ inch stick cinnamon
100 g coarse semolina or ground rice	4 oz coarse semolina or ground rice
1.2 litres milk	2 pints milk
175 g sugar	6 oz sugar
25 g sultanas	1 oz sultanas
10–15 small green cardamoms, shelled and seeds ground	10–15 small green cardamoms, shelled and seeds ground
25 g blanched almonds, sliced or chopped	1 oz blanched almonds, sliced or chopped

Preparation time: 10 minutes
Cooking time: 1 hour

A kheer, or payasam, is very similar to a milk pudding and it is the most popular sweet dish in India. It can also be made with sago or rice vermicelli and flavoured with rose water, kewra water, saffron, coconut milk, or vanilla. Sliced fruits such as banana, mango, apple, orange or dates, can also be added when the kheer has cooled.

In a heavy-based or nonstick pan, melt the ghee or butter. Add the cinnamon and fry for ½ minute. Add the semolina or rice and half of the milk, and stir. Cover and cook for 15–20 minutes until soft. Mash the mixture, then stir in the sugar and the remaining milk. Simmer gently for 20–25 minutes stirring constantly to prevent the kheer sticking to the base of the pan. By this time the kheer should be thick. Add the sultanas and check for sweetness. If the kheer is too thick, add a little extra milk or water and cook gently for 5–6 minutes.
Remove from the heat and pour into a serving dish. Stir in the ground cardamom and decorate with nuts. This can be served hot or cold and is especially good if chilled in the refrigerator before serving.

Variations:
When using coarse semolina or ground rice a deliciously mild toffee flavour can be achieved by using this method. Boil the milk until it has reduced by one quarter. Add the rice and sugar and cook for 15 minutes, stirring occasionally. Any grains of rice that slightly stick to the base of the pan will produce a light brown result and the mild toffee flavour. Stir in the ground cardamom and sultanas. Remove from the heat and cover. Decorate with nuts.
To add flavourings such as rose or kewra water, stir in 3–4 drops when the kheer has cooled.

Baisen barfi (chick pea flour fudge)

Metric	Imperial
350 g unsalted butter or ghee	12 oz unsalted butter or ghee
275 g baisen flour, sifted	10 oz baisen flour, sifted
300 ml water	½ pint water
350 g sugar	12 oz sugar
pinch of salt	pinch of salt
10 small green cardamoms, shelled and seeds ground	10 small green cardamoms, shelled and seeds ground
30 g mixed unsalted nuts, sliced, e.g. almonds, pistachio and cashew nuts	1¼ oz mixed unsalted nuts, sliced, e.g. almonds, pistachio and cashew nuts

Preparation time: 15 minutes
Cooking time: 25–30 minutes

Baisen flour is popular in Indian cooking and can be bought from Asian food stores. Take care when frying it because although the flour must be thoroughly cooked to avoid any raw flavour, it also burns easily.

Grease a 20 × 25 cm/8 × 10 inch baking dish. Using a nonstick or a heavy-based pan, melt the butter or ghee and gently fry the baisen flour for 5–6 minutes, stirring constantly, until light brown. Remove from the heat.
Prepare a thick sugar syrup by placing the water in a saucepan with the sugar. Heat until the sugar dissolves, then bring to the boil for 5 minutes until the syrup is light golden and has thickened. If a small spoonful is taken out and cooled slightly it should form a single strand between the finger and thumb. If the syrup becomes too thick add a little water.
Add the fried baisen to the syrup and cook on a low heat for 10–15 minutes, stirring constantly, until the mixture comes away from the sides of the pan and forms a ball. Remove from the heat, stir in the salt, ground cardamom and nuts. Pour into the greased dish and smooth the surface with a wet spatula. Cool and cut into cubes or diamond shapes.

From the left, clockwise: Shrikhand; Baisen barfi; Chawal ki kheer

Shrikhand
(yogurt pudding)

Metric
450 g curd cheese
100 g full fat soft
   cheese
150 ml plain unsweetened
   yogurt
100–175 g icing sugar
10–15 small green
   cardamoms, shelled
   and seeds ground
pinch of ground
   saffron

To decorate:
25 g blanched almonds,
   sliced
15 g pistachio nuts,
   sliced

Imperial
1 lb curd cheese
4 oz full fat soft
   cheese
1/4 pint plain unsweetened
   yogurt
4–6 oz icing sugar
10–15 small green
   cardamoms, shelled
   and seeds ground
pinch of ground
   saffron

To decorate:
1 oz blanched almonds,
   sliced
1/2 oz pistachio nuts,
   sliced

Preparation time: 15 minutes

In a mixing bowl, beat the cheeses and yogurt until a smooth consistency. Gradually add the sugar and continue beating until light and fluffy. Stir in the ground cardamoms and saffron with a metal spoon. Pour into one dish or individual serving dishes and decorate with the sliced nuts. Chill before serving.

Variation:
A more authentic but more time consuming method uses 1 litre/1¾ pints plain unsweetened yogurt instead of the curd cheese. Tie the yogurt in a muslin bag and leave overnight until all the liquid has seeped through into a large bowl. Add the full fat soft cheese, gradually beat in the sugar and complete as before.

INDEX

PDO 82-1413